"Life is a journey, bringing both good and bad in our direction. While we can't control what comes our way, we do control our reaction. Using the tools that Andrea shares in her marvelous book *I Am Resilient*, the reader will learn how to increase in hope even when it looks like the end. Watching Andrea's life and seeing how she lives is inspiring. And we believe that you too can live a life of resilience."

Bill and Beni Johnson
Bethel Church
Authors of *God is Good* and *Healthy and Free*

"Perhaps nobody has the ability to show you how to make it through the wilderness and come out in the Promised Land like Andrea Thompson. This book shows you how to count it all joy when you face various trials while giving you the steps to use your challenges as tools to fulfill your destiny."

Dr. Ben Lerner, NY Times Best-Selling Author of *Body by God*.

"Andrea Thompson is one of the most inspirational and influential leaders of today. An individual that is a true example of making positive choices and change when adversity and illness came knocking at her own door with the dreaded diagnosis of cancer. Andrea now uses her life experiences and her successes in conquering them to educate others in the areas of positive mindset, healthy eating, and lifestyle medicine as they seek guidance on better ways of living. Andrea is very passionate about health and meshes her professional healthcare and ministry backgrounds into the emotional, mental, and spiritual aspects of whole person wellness with great effectiveness. Andrea Thompson is definitely a person to watch and follow in the future."

Dr. Sonja L. O'Bryan, Pharm.D., ABAAHP
Board Certified Healthcare Practitioner Diplomate
American Academy of Anti-Aging Medicine
Hormones/Adrenal/Thyroid/Fatigue/Weight
Management/Nutraceuticals/Wellness Consulting

"Andrea is a woman of childlike faith with dogged determination to not be denied. She knows what it means to be lifted up by the grace of God and then use that same grace to lift you up. If you need some practical "how to's" to take control of your health and prosperity of soul, this book is for you."

Diane Bickle
International House of Prayer, Kansas City

"What a powerhouse of inspiration, strength and courage. Andrea Thompson exudes all of these characteristics and to be able to call her friend has been truly a gift."

Kimmee Auxier
Auxier Family Farms, LLC
Auxier Ranch

"Andrea's testimony and her passion for health have been a huge inspiration. She has not only inspired me, but her wisdom and insight in nutrition and wellness have helped me to implement healthy, sustainable changes in my lifestyle. I am truly grateful for her."

Ray Leight
Author of *Identity Restoration*

"Our relationship with Andrea is a little unusual. My wife, Linda, and I have felt blessed to have a large enough house to be able to offer some space for friends and family during some of life's transition times. Andrea and her daughter, Hunter, found themselves in such a place several years ago. Andrea found her way to our basement at a critical point in her life. I think it was more of a God found Andrea a safe place to grow and then to blossom. Our youngest daughter, Shani, called us while we were out of the country on vacation to tell us that Andrea needed a place to stay ... now! We said, "Yes, absolutely." Andrea spent most of our early home time crying. We spent most of the first couple of months just listening; being there. We included Andrea and Hunter in all things "family." Effective immediately, they were part of the family. During the next two years, we laughed and cried but it moved to more laughing and less crying as time went by. It was not an easy process but as Andrea immersed herself in 'study of the Bible,' we watched a very dynamic woman come to life. We were thrilled when her husband Joe entered the picture. It added permanent stability to her life. Andrea's journey has given her a unique and invaluable opportunity to connect with people from every walk of life. Regardless of where we live or how much money is in our bank account, we are all presented challenges in our earthly walk. Finding The Higher Power and your inner strength makes all the difference in how you are able to navigate life's rough waters. God's work is getting done in a big way through Andrea's ability to share her lessons learned. We love seeing what is happening. We have so enjoyed being a part of her life."

Mike Brown

"Andrea has been such blessing to me, my wife, and my ministry. She is a leader who builds up people, organizations, and churches. She and her ministry are contagious!"

Dr. Barry Young
Founder of Serving Pastors, Chaplain for
Independence, Missouri Police Department

"Andrea is amazing! I was recently diagnosed with diabetes after having a blood glucose reading of over 600 and as a result was given metformin and insulin. I was upset especially because the insulin has so many nasty side effects. I went to Andrea for help and with her advice she put me on a nutrition plan as well as natural supplements. In less than a month I was off the insulin and taking a smaller dose of metformin and my blood glucose has been less than 100 consistently my goal is that by mid-2018 I'll be off the metformin and maintaining my sugar levels naturally. Thank you, Andrea, for your guidance, God bless!"

USA Retired Guadalupe Mendez

"We are all on a journey, in process, which ultimately makes up our life. In this book Andrea puts words to that process. She gives a unique insight and meaning into a word that I have overlooked, "resilience." Instead of just a book you read, Andrea takes you on a journey with practical applications, this gives opportunity for you to ask yourself questions. Andrea helps to articulate how God is there in the process. Much like Andrea's real life experiences, this book will inspire hope in the midst of your challenges."

Jon Cook
Projects Director, Bethel Church

"This girl knows her stuff! Andrea Thompson has the Amazing ability to bring you to a place of believing in the unbelievable for yourself! When it comes to complete healing – body, soul, mind and spirit–she has it on lockdown! Because she carries personal breakthrough in every one of these areas you can feel the authority she carries! Hands down the Best!"

Jenna Winston

"I have watched Satan come against Andrea many times. Each time God helped her go through. Her faith got stronger each time. Words can't describe how it makes me feel watching these victories and seeing what God has done for her. I am so Blessed to know her and her husband!"

Danny and Happy Sparks
Lafayette Foster and Adoptive Support

"A friend of mine suggested that I talk to Andrea about some health issues that I had been sharing with her. I had been to many doctors and even been in the hospital trying to figure out what was happening inside my body. The doctors were clueless and did not suggest anything other than over the counter drugs. That was not an option for me! After spending just an hour with Andrea on the phone, she had laid out a clear plan to find the issue, and then address it. She recommended me to get some tests done, and we discovered that I was severely low in progesterone, DHEA, testosterone, as well had been suffering with a Candida overgrowth that was causing all the issues! Andrea helped me adjust my diet, my mindset, was able to recommend supplements, and helped me find natural ways to address each of the issues! Andrea not only offered practical strategies to help me overcome these health issues, but she prayed with me, and helped me address unhealthy mindsets in my thinking pattern with health! A huge bonus was that I lost 11 pounds in two weeks following her recommendations, not to mention I have begun to feel so much better! Andrea is a GOD send! And her journey to overcome obstacles and live in divine health has blessed me tremendously!"

Rebekah White
Worship Singer/Songwriter
Nashville, TN

"Andrea's authentic, Jesus-centered encouragement has been an invaluable blessing in my life. Her passion for truth and wholeness propel her ministry that continues to impact my life and countless others."

Robin Cook
Nourish2Flourish.com **Health Coach**
Author of *Cook2Flourish*

"When you get around Andrea you are suddenly inspired to live a healthy life! I can't really explain why but Andrea because of what she's been through personally in her life carries an atmosphere of hope and determination to live your life healthy by eating well, taking great vitamins, and staying close to God. I trust her with my health, and I want the world to know her and her health wisdom!! She's a key to future generations healthy living!"

Inga-Mae Carlin

"When my husband and I met Andrea, she was an emotionally and spiritually broken young woman who needed a chance to reinvent herself. While we provided her with stability and love, she began a journey that would change not only her life, but the lives of others. Always searching, always learning, she has found her true self, through faith and love and healing, and has the unwavering desire to share her story with others who also seek to find the meaning and purpose in their lives that she has found in hers."

Linda Brown

"I have been impressed by Andrea's intentionality with every aspect of her health. She has more than just overcome, she has brought others along with her. She lives what she shares and does so with joy and grace. I appreciate Andrea's humor as she conquers even the toughest obstacles.

She is a woman who knows what she is about and doesn't settle for less than what God has for her."

Kathryn Leight
Identity Coach, Faith by Grace Ministries
Pastoral Counselor, Bethel Transformation Center

"This book put words to my life that I was not able to articulate before, especially when Andrea talked about resilience. I was filled with so much emotion as I read; it was as if her journey connected with my rough and very unsafe childhood. I was consumed with emotion as I realized that resilience played a very large role in my life. I was so overwhelmed with the awareness of the reality of how much God was with me in my life and process. This book will connect with your heart and your life it has brought me so much truth."

Zerlene Cook
Bethel Church

"My friend, Andrea Thompson, addresses a subject that we all have had to navigate at opportune and inopportune times in our life — Resilience! This subject is powerful, and so is Andrea. Through her stories and collection of testimonies, you'll find a new alignment with God's pleasure and purpose in your ability to consistently rise to the occasion and display His unbelievable power at work in us. We all walk through tough times, and I have witnessed Andrea fight the good fight up close and personal. She knows what she's talking about! This book reveals the insider perspective we all need to blueprint our behavior and show ourselves 'mature and complete, not lacking anything.' If you want to truly understand Resilience and how God defines the kingdom expression of it, then pick up your copy of *I Am Resilient*. It's a game-changer for how you live your life and use your resources to get the most out of every challenge and difficulty that comes your way."

Mary Hawblitzel

"Daniel Chalmers and I have had the joy and honor of knowing Andrea Thompson for the past two years. Our lives are so much richer through this friendship. As a health coach, Andrea sacrificially sowed into and served me when I got so ill from a vanishing twin during pregnancy that I did not think I could travel to the Sundance Film Festival. I was fainting, light headed, throwing up ten times a day, and even laying on the ground in church with heart palpitations. Within 72 hours of her wisdom and care, I was so remarkably better and did not throw up once at the week-long festival in high altitudes. She is an emerging voice in our generation. With a profound and powerful personal testimony of overcoming trauma, being healed from cancer, coupled with professional training in health, as well as her rich deep history in the Lord, she is the embodiment of her book - she is resilient through and through. Andrea's very life testifies that when God restores something, it's greater than the original. Nothing is impossible for the One who exchanges beauty for ashes and sets us all as His trophies of grace. This book, *I Am Resilient* carries keys that took decades for her to earn. May you go on a journey of encountering the heart of the father as you read the pages that lie before you … Andrea has labored a lifetime for the chapters that await you! Each chapter cost her and is written from her own blood, sweat and tears. And the spoils of her victory become ours. Her breakthrough is contagious. Her testimony is our invitation. We believe she will one day be like a Joyce Meyer by speaking globally to God's people about physical healing — spirit, soul, and body. As you read, may you put a full demand on heaven to receive everything Jesus died for!"

Shara and Daniel Chalmers
Love Wins Ministries

I Am Resilient

12 traits to help you live confident,
empowered and fully alive!

ANDREA THOMPSON
Cancer, abuse and life overcomer

andreathompson.org
iamresilient.net
fromcancertovictory.com

Cover photos provided by: Heather Armstrong
heatherarmstrongphotography.com

Makeup provided by: Rachel McKnew

Thank you

Jesus Christ - first and foremost for without Him I would not be here today. Thank you for saving and redeeming my life.

Joe - my husband, biggest supporter, advocate and love of my life.

My children - for loving me and supporting me no matter what.

Jon Essen - without whom this book would not be possible. Thank you for the countless hours, excellence and pulling out the best in me.

Lindsay Snyder - your skills are incredible, and I am so grateful for your passion, servant-heart and all our brilliant meetings at Barnes and Noble. You really are a gift.

Friends - who became family and wise counsel for me, who believed in me and what God was doing in my life from the very of humblest beginnings, and helped champion my dreams, vision and desires.

Mike, Linda and Shani - who gave me a place to live when I had no where to go and, in that basement, resilience was being developed in me.

Pastor Barry Young - who saw resilience in me when I walked into his office back in 2007 completely broken, gave me a chance, and helped me walk it out with such grace and love.

Contents

Just for You

I believe you can make it through anything in life and I believe it so much that I want to take you on a journey, a journey of becoming resilient.

The truth is Resilience doesn't have a face, a body type, a race or gender. Resilience has a story. Resilience loves to take your story and turn it around for the win. It's like the backbone of your comeback.

Resilience is what kept Corrie ten Boom in a place of faith during Nazi Holocaust imprisonment and led a boxer like Rocky Balboa to defy the odds and public opinions of others in order to overcome.

My name is Andrea Thompson. I have learned that through the hardest times of my life I have become what I didn't know I already was, resilient.

And it's a gift God wants you to discover too.

I don't know where you are right now, but I want you to know that I am here for you and I want to help.

The best part of your life is still in front of you, and it's time for you to pursue it! It's time for you to declare "I Am Resilent."

Andrea Thompson

Write It Down

In places throughout the book, you'll have a chance to respond to various questions. Some are found within the content of the chapters, and some are at the end of each chapter, in a proactive takeaway section I am calling "1-2 it's up to you."

While it would be easy to just answer in your mind and perhaps make a mental list, I want to encourage you to take it to the next level.

Write it down. Answer the questions on paper, or within the book itself, or make notes on your computer or smartphone.

I can't emphasize enough how vitally important it is to actually write down your reactions, goals or insights.

It puts it in front of you, and it will make all the difference in your journey.

A Resilient Person's New Formula

How to Set Your Life for Success

Chapter 1

▼

"I don't know if I can handle this again."

With a bloodied face and tired soul, I muttered these words to myself.

It had been a while since I had was abused by the hands of men. But at this moment, my pain and my physical wounds weren't coming from someone abusing me, rather they were coming because I had chosen to fight.

After spending years of living in extreme defeat in what seemed like every area of my life, as an outlet to learn some self-control (and how to protect myself), I devoted myself to an intense, disciplined martial art called Taekwondo.

On one particular day, I was competing in a tournament, sparring against some of the best talent in the country.

I was assigned to a sparring match against a spirited young woman, who, I admit, initially got the best of me.

But as I lay on the mat and tried to regain my strength and my composure, I was suddenly overwhelmed by the feeling that I had a decision to make.

I could either walk away from months of training, or, I could risk failure, rise, and fight again.

My opponent stood in the center of the ring, waiting for me to indicate my next move. I made a decision that day that wasn't about martial arts, it was about a way of thinking that would radically change my future.

I crossed the line, stepped back into the ring, and decided to face my opposition head-on.

Resilience: What Is It?

The concept of resilience is as old as mankind. There are countless stories woven throughout history of people who didn't back down, even when the odds were against them.

In my case, and within the intensity of my life story, resilience was something that I didn't quite know how to grasp.

Resilience wasn't just about willpower, and it definitely wasn't all about being stronger or tougher (physically or emotionally) than someone else.

I had an incredible discovery as to what resilience was – and it came through an unlikely "teacher."

All Creation Loves to Speak

It was winter in Kansas City, MO as I sat at my kitchen table, snow falling about an inch an hour as I stared out the window at the enormous snowflakes.

My eyes were drawn to one particular branch that hung from my favorite oak tree. The wet snow was beginning to pile up and weigh down the branch; it looked as though it was going to break at any moment.

But then the branch began to slowly contort downward as if it were bending over to allow the snow to literally fall off.

This scene had my complete attention. As the branch dumped the heavy snow, it immediately sprung back into place still in one piece. I was surprised. To be honest, I was sure the branch would give under the weight of the snow and break off from the tree. But it didn't.

The snowflakes piled on top of each other, one after another, descending rapidly at times.

It reminded me of how quickly the issues of life can accumulate.

The branch was resilient.

Resilience is the ability of a substance or object to spring back to its original shape after it has been pulled, stretched, pressed or bent. It's the capacity to recover quickly from difficulties.

If tree branches were intentionally created with the ability to make such a comeback, how much more intentionally were we created?

Let me pause quickly and tell you the secret sauce that has revolutionized my life. I have to unapologetically share the truth that I love God and I love His Word. God and His Word are why I am alive today.

Now if God is not on your radar that is ok—don't think you can't continue with this book.

He wasn't on mine either, until He was.

I am not here to convince you that God is real. I found that He does a pretty good job of that Himself. I want to let you know that I honor whatever you believe, but you will hear me talk about God from time to time in this book.

God knew we would encounter various trials in life, the Bible even says so. It's interesting what is in the Bible. It says we were created in such a way that we could overcome the proverbial snowflakes of life with this thing called resilience.

For so many years of my life, I was striving and fighting to survive. I thought if I didn't fight, I wouldn't make it; I thought it was all up to me.

But as I have come to know more about the truth of who I am, I have learned to change my mind about who is doing what. That may sound odd but stay with me here.

I now realize that I needed to change my mind and the rest would take care of itself, like a trickle-down effect.

I remember it was a typical Saturday afternoon and I was drinking my favorite ginger turmeric green tea when an article came across my computer screen from the *Harvard Business Review*. It contained a question that impacted my life profoundly: "What exactly is that quality of resilience that carries people through life?"[1]

"That's a good question," I asked myself. "What exactly is resilience?"

The article went on to say that "Resilience is one of the great puzzles of human nature, like creativity, or the religious instinct."[2]

"Yes, exactly, it's a puzzle!" I said to myself. "But what are the pieces that make up that puzzle?"

At first, the answer seemed simple. *It's obvious. It's good old-fashioned hard work plus some grit your teeth determination"* and there you have it, I thought.

I mean that is what I learned from my old taekwondo instructor. She would say "Andrea, pull the pacifier out of your mouth and get out there and do it."

And she was right, that is exactly what worked for me.

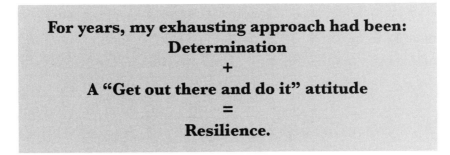

For years, my exhausting approach had been:
Determination
+
A "Get out there and do it" attitude
=
Resilience.

I was sure this had to be it.

That was until one day I heard the still small voice of God, "Andrea, you can rest."

When I heard God tell me I could rest, I thought that was insane—crazy even.

"I need to go out there and get it done; that is what winners do and that is what I have had to do all my life," I responded.

But then that still small voice whispered back, "Andrea, there is a better way. Let me show you."

Cancer and Rest

When I was diagnosed with cervical cancer and given about a year to live, I knew I was in a real fight for my life. It was interesting how part of the protocol for my healing was allowing my body to rest. There it was again, that word rest.

I was told by the experts that fighting for my life was about letting my body rest. That was going to be hard for me because I was not wired that way. I was not a sit still kind of girl.

I also learned I didn't know what real rest looked like.

Rest, in that season, meant meditating on God's Word; it meant putting on my music and doing things that took my mind off the present situation. Resting meant speaking life over myself even though everything around me was speaking death including the medical professionals. I very vividly remember the moment the doc said, "You have a year at best."

That's when it became real and the fight for my life began; it just didn't happen the way I thought. I distinctly remember the kind voice of God saying to me, "Andrea, do you believe me or not? Do you believe what My Word says or not?"

And that's when Romans 12:2 became my life verse, literally the verse that brought me life. If you aren't familiar with that scripture, I am here to help you. Check this out:

"And do not be conformed to this world, but be transformed by the renewing of your mind, so that you may prove what the will of God is, that which is good and acceptable and perfect."

I had to renew my very thought process, and what the world was saying could no longer matter.

I wasn't going to align with what the world said anymore; they were saying things like "you are going to die" and "you are going to be in so much agony." I had to decide who I was going to agree with, God or the world.

I had to renew my very thought process, and what the world was saying could no longer matter.

Fighting from a place of rest was possible because I was fighting with the Sword of the Spirit, the very Word of God; It is said to deflect every flaming arrow of the enemy.

Words of death could no longer penetrate the words of life I had discovered in my Bible. I had to choose to believe the words of life. I had to learn how to create an environment of life.

I realized I didn't have to engage in this fight from a place of panic, chaos or disappointment because God had given me the tools and resources I needed. He had given me wisdom and knowledge of how to do it. And I had to choose to do it.

Is Resilience a Choice?

That's a good question. The choice of resilience is about identity, about believing who we are. And it has more to do with identity than one might think.

It's important to this process.

I tried for many years to do things according to my own willpower, and let me tell you, I have a lot of personal willpower. But willpower would only take me so far. I needed something outside myself to not only survive but also to thrive.

The question usually becomes, how heavy do things have to get in order for us to release the weight of our circumstances? And a good question is, who are you going to release those circumstances to?

If we are born with resilience in our DNA, why is it that some people overcome, and others don't?

What is it that makes the difference?

That's the question which kept me awake at night; that's what I wanted to know; that's why I went on this journey.

What's the Problem?

Hara Marano writes about the mentality of resilience in her article "The Art of Resilience" for *Psychology Today.com*:

> There are elements of our culture that glorify frailty, says Washington, D.C. psychiatrist Steven Wolin, M.D. There is a whole industry that would turn you into a victim by having you dwell on the traumas in your life. In reality you have considerable capacity for strength, although you might not be wholly aware of it.
>
> Sometimes it is easier to be a victim; talking about how other people make you do what you do removes the obligation to

change. And sympathy can feel sweet; talk of resilience can make some feel that no one is really appreciating exactly how much they have suffered.

Wolin defines resiliency as the capacity to rise above adversity—sometimes the terrible adversity of outright violence, molestation or war—and can forge lasting strengths in the struggle. It is the means by which children of troubled families are not immobilized by hardship but rebound from it, learn to protect themselves and emerge as strong adults, able to lead gratifying lives.[3]

I remember being at my cousin's wedding when my uncle, a psychiatrist, said to me, "Hey, tell me about your book." He was referring to my first book in which I tell my life story. As I was going through the bullet points of my story he said, "Wow, you are resilient!"

I responded, "Huh?"

He just looked at me and said, "I am truly amazed at what you are doing."

It was what he said next that marked me and changed the way I thought about myself. He said, "Andrea, I am a psychiatrist who prescribes medication to people daily and have been for forty plus years, but what you are doing is changing people's lives in a way I could never do with a single drug or all the counseling in the world. You are resilient."

I had never really used the word resilient. I had never thought of myself as resilient, and you may not either.

But the truth is, you are!

You were born with resilience in your blood.

You bought this book.

You have overcome hard things.

And learning to activate even more resilience in your life is going to be powerful.

Dean Becker, the President and CEO of Adaptiv Learning Systems, who develops and delivers programs about resilience training, puts it this way: "More than education, more than experience, more than training, a person's level of resilience will determine who succeeds and who fails. That's true in the cancer ward, it's true in the Olympics, and it's true in the boardroom."[4]

What Does it Take?

Awareness is key when it comes to understanding who you are and what you are truly made of. You need to know what you think you are because setbacks are a part of life, Jesus even told us that in scripture. Setbacks set you up for your greatest comeback.

What do I mean by "who you are"?

One of the greatest lessons of my life was going from being a victim to a victor. Victor sounds like an odd word, but it means one who is already victorious. It is who we are rather than what we do.

Let's face it, you're still here. You made it to where you are, and that is a victory to be celebrated.

Valorie Burton, founder of The Coaching and Positive Psychology Institute, says:

It's hard to bounce back from setbacks when you see every obstacle as the end of the world! Research shows that optimists live as much as nine years longer than pessimists. Seeing the bright side is good for your health and longevity. But it isn't about simplistic "positive thinking." Resilient people see risks and take precautions to prevent problems. But when faced with a challenge, they are more likely to say, "I can get through this," whether it is a test, a divorce or the loss of a loved one.[5]

Resilience is not a synonym of toughness, it is a response of hope. If you kill hope, resilience dies with it.

There are two kinds of hope. One is the hope that the world gives to us—the wishy-washy kind of hope, the wishful thinking that says, "I hope this to be the case, but I am not sure if it's even possible. And then we set ourselves up by making an already predetermined excuse when it doesn't happen." I call those walls that we build to deflect disappointment.

This kind of hope is a wish with nothing behind it, nothing anchoring it, "Oh. I wish that would happen."

Proverbs 13:12 states, *"Hope deferred makes the heart sick..."*

The second kind of hope is the Hope of Jesus Christ. It is a "know so" kind of hope; I "know so because God said so" kind of hope. In Romans 4:18, it says of Abraham, *"In hope against hope he believed, so that he might become a father of many nations..."*

The moment we disconnect, usually due to the distraction of circumstances, trauma, or issues of life, we lose sight of who we are, and more importantly, whose we are, and we stop believing and lose our strength. Our source of strength comes from God;

we may get halfway through on our own, but then we will run out of strength and need Him to carry us the rest of the way.

"Resilience is the ability to work with adversity in such a way that one comes through it unharmed or even better for the experience."
– Unknown

Resilience means facing life's difficulties with courage, hope and strength, refusing to give up. It is the quality of character that allows a person or group of people to rebound from misfortune, hardships or traumas.

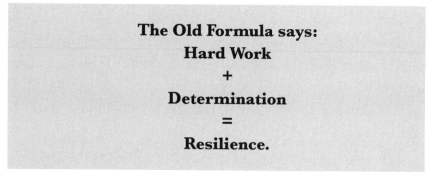

The Old Formula says:
Hard Work
+
Determination
=
Resilience.

While this approach can give you certain "results", I discovered (the hard way) that it led to ongoing burnout, disappointment, unhealthy comparisons to others, and most importantly, long-term defeat.

So let me offer an alternative that has revolutionized my life.

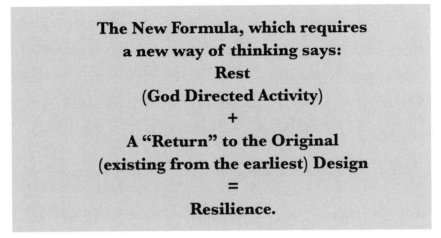

**The New Formula, which requires
a new way of thinking says:
Rest
(God Directed Activity)
+
A "Return" to the Original
(existing from the earliest) Design
=
Resilience.**

A return to the original design begins with the mind.

As someone once said, "where our mind goes, the rest of us is sure to follow."

We will talk about the act of renewing the mind over the course of this book. It is about resetting your mind to the original design.

It's an ongoing process, it's a journey that we are about to embark on together.

I can't wait to continue this journey together...

▶

1-2 it's up to you!

Resilient Thought:
Resilience means facing life's difficulties with courage, hope and strength, refusing to give up. It is the quality of character that allows you to rebound from misfortune, hardships or traumas, and positions you to overcome.

1) What areas are you feeling like need resilience in your own life?

2) How can you take your first step today in any of these areas?

A Resilient Person Knows Which End is Up

How to Know Your "Why" ▶

Real Life Scenario

Pam was tired and confused. It had been almost two years since she committed to volunteer coaching for her daughter's volleyball team, and she was still working two "half-to-three-quarter-time" jobs in order to make ends meet. Pam was an incredibly smart and talented individual. A long-time athlete, Pam graduated college with a business degree, got married and started the "life of her dreams." As time went by, her marriage began to erode and eventually led to divorce. She found herself doing everything she could to prove to others (and herself) that she could survive. But over time she found that working just to pay bills each month began to drain her emotions, as much as it did her physical energy. On top of that, she was being asked to volunteer at her church. Pam loved to help and serve o thers, but she was experiencing a lifestyle that she didn't know what to do with, or how to navigate.

Chapter 2

▼

I don't know how many of you have ever taken flying lessons, but there is a unique similarity between the cockpit of an airplane and the inner workings of our soul.

In the cockpit of every airplane there are two of the exact same gauges. These gauges literally tell the pilot which end of the airplane is up. Under certain conditions the pilot may be deprived of an external visual horizon, which is critical to maintaining a correct sense of up and down while flying. A pilot who enters such conditions will quickly lose spatial orientation if there has been no training in flying with reference to instruments.

There are two of the exact same gauges in each airplane. This is to bring confidence to the pilot. If both gauges say "up" it is very likely they are right and the pilot's feelings, if different, are wrong.

We often hear things like "trust your gut," but in this scenario, it is about trusting the instruments that have been put there as a guide for you to get to your intended destination.

When I heard this story, it reminded me of life; it reminded me of times when I thought I was going in one direction, but I was heading in the exact opposite direction of where I wanted to go. When it comes to the choices we make in life, wouldn't it be nice if we had a gauge that would reassure with "this is the right way" or "this is the right decision?"

But you and I both know it doesn't work that way. We don't have a gauge in front of our face that we can read and know without a doubt we are making the right "turn" in life. It is up to us to figure it out.

And it may not be as hard as you think.

There is a gauge that we can bring into our everyday lives that will help show the way.

It's actually the first step toward becoming a resilient person.

It's called knowing your "why."

Because once you know your why, it will make seeing your way so much easier, clearer and more purposeful.

It sounds simple, but without this being at the foundation of our journey, we may get off course. Just like a map on a hike through a mountain, without knowing where you are going or why you are doing it, you may very well end up going in the wrong direction and end up at an undesired location.

The good news is, you can turn around at any point in life, unlike the pilot that may head in the wrong direction and find out too late. You may hit rock bottom in life, but a resilient person gets back up and starts again.

That is the brilliance of life. You're not done until you are truly done. You can set a new course for your life at any time—a new destination—and begin walking that way. It is never too late.

The map you choose will be up to you. And your destination will depend on your goals, wants and desires.

What is your desired destination? It's a question we all have to ask ourselves.

But before we get to that question, we need to step back and look at why we want to go that way.

> **That is the brilliance of life. You're not done until you are truly done. You can set a new course for your life at any time—a new destination—and begin walking that way. It is never too late.**

Your why is going to help you reach your goal, and step by step you will make it to your desired destination.

The Reason for Your Motivation

It is said that physical therapy is 60% physiological and 40% physical. In my 30's I went back to school to be a Physical Therapist. Why? Well, I was a single mom with two kids working all kinds of rinky-dink jobs. I was tired of it and I wanted something better for myself and my kids.

So, I made a decision to learn about the "whys" of life.

I found that every person I worked with—whether an athlete or an elderly person in a skilled nursing facility—had to have a "why."

If I was working with someone who wasn't motivated, it was my job to figure out the one thing that was going to motivate him or her to get up and move.

For the athlete, it was often the desire to play the next game or another season.

When I would meet with my athlete, I would remind him of his why. I would say, "Johnny, you can do this! Remember, if you keep going, you will be ready for next season." I would then see him use all his strength to take the next step.

The skilled nursing facility was somewhat the same, but sadly the majority of people in there were just waiting to die. They didn't have much hope. But again, it was my job to figure out the one thing I could do to motivate them and get them out of bed.

I spent a great deal of time building relationships with my patients in order to figure out their why's. Often, motivation came from personal reasons like "I want to be able to see my granddaughter walk down the aisle."

There it is, the "why."

From that point, every time we would meet I would say, "Alright Margret, we are going to get up today so that you will be ready for that wedding in June." A smile would often come across her face, and she would use all her strength to walk down the hallway. Margret was doing it for a reason; she remembered her why.

Both the athlete and the elderly woman had their why's in mind as they overcame feelings of "I can't" and pushed into believing they could. And guess what? They did.

And so can you.

Resilience is learning how to bounce back from challenges and adversity. Grabbing onto your why in the midst of those challenges will propel you forward.

Without resilience, you will be tempted to see yourself as a victim and feel overwhelmed by debilitating hopelessness.

C. Kavin Rowe, Professor at Duke Divinity School, says, "The first way to cultivate resilience … is to recalibrate our imagination to the reality of profound difficulty as a natural part of life."[6]

In simple terms, this means we can actually grow from our life challenges.

Rowe is not saying this to deter us but rather to help us understand that we are not alone in our struggles and "this" is not just happening to us. When I look at all the hard stuff in my life and think *poor me*, I am headed straight for the prison of self-pity.

We were designed as overcomers in Christ Jesus, and that's one reason I know my need for Him. I need and want all the help I can get in overcoming what comes my way in life.

God knew there would be things to overcome in this world, so He created us this way. It's not just what we do, it is literally who we are; it is part of our identity.

Are Challenges Only Physical?

No, the challenges we face in life are not just physical, they are deeply emotional as well. The emotional issues of life can seem even harder to spot because they aren't always obvious.

But there is One who knows it all.

The Word of God tells us that the Holy Spirit of God was sent to live inside of us. This is a good thing! He doesn't come to dwell in you to point out all the wrong things in your life. He comes to help us work through and overcome the difficulties that are coming against us. He is referred to most often as the "Counselor" or the "Helper." Who doesn't need a helper or a counselor in life? I know I do.

We will talk later in the book about having community and what a friend of mine refers to as the Strong Team around you to help you through things. But I would propose that you have one of those already inside of you, the wisest One of all, the Holy Spirit, the Spirit of God Himself.

Scripture says in the book of James that if *we ask for wisdom, He (meaning God) will give it to us generously*. What a promise!

He also says that He gives it to us *without finding fault* in our asking. This is such great news because, like me, there have probably been countless times where you charged into something without asking for God's help.

His promise is that He gives it, and our past decisions and circumstances don't stop Him from continuing to lavish it on us. We just have to ask.

Your Goals and Your Why

Knowing your why will help you make decisions, much like having a map at your disposal on a road trip.

There was a trip I had an opportunity to go on and it was something I was deeply passionate about. It was going to be fun. All kinds of people I loved were going and I wanted to go too. But my super supportive husband asked me, "Andrea, does this line up with your recent goals for helping people overcome in health and in life?"

Hmmmmm, I thought. He was right. It really didn't.

Could I have gone and had a great time? No doubt it would have been a blast, but it didn't line up with my goals.

If I hadn't known my desired destination, I would have had a hard time figuring out whether that trip was going to lead me closer or set me off course a bit.

> **Knowing your why will help you make decisions, much like having a map at your disposal on a road trip.**

Understanding your why is arguably one of the most important parts of the journey to overcoming in any area of your life.

Let's Do It

It's simple and I know you can do it. Below are some good questions to ask yourself to help define your why. Take a moment to write down your answers.

"What do I want to accomplish?"

"What inspires me and makes me come alive?"

"What am I willing to let go of?"

"What would a dream life look like to me?"

Next, complete this sentence:

The reason I exist is to_____ and I will accomplish it by _____. My ability to say "yes" or "no" is strengthened because I am committed to _____.

This is your mission and you now have a goal. Great job!

Through goals we begin to prioritize. And goal setting is a skill, so don't be overwhelmed. We get good at it through practice.

I personally love doing this exercise with the Counselor. The One who lives inside of us is a gift that Jesus gave to all those who believe in Him. You can have Him too; He is a great help.

To overcome is a choice. Believe it or not, to stay a victim of your past or current circumstances is also a choice. Being resilient is learned through experience.

It's only in challenge or adversity that we get to see ourselves as being resilient.

You Can Change the Way You Think

When it comes to obstacles in life, an unhealthy mindset sounds something like this, "I just can't do it because (insert excuse)." An excuse feels very real to you—there is no condemnation for how you feel—but you must be honest with yourself, so you can overcome.

Choose to change your mindset. Remember it's a choice. Choose to say instead, "I can _____ because _____!"

For example, I can *go back to school* because *I want to continue to earn my degree so that I can move upward in my career*!

In Philippians 4:13, Paul states that *"I can do all things through Him who strengthens me."* This is exactly how I have walked through the hardest circumstances in my life from a true place of rest. I have asked for His strength.

Vision, Purpose, and Passion

When you understand your why, you are creating vision, purpose and passion toward your end goals. You are also giving yourself permission to say "yes" to the right things and "no" to the things that are not taking you in your desired direction.

Understanding and continually clarifying your why will keep you motivated and from giving up so that you can experience the life you were meant to live.

When I don't know my why and my direction, I find myself in a place of chaos and unrest because I am trying to strive for whatever seems right as opposed to when I know my why, it grounds me. It keeps me from going here and there.

Knowing my why helps me find my center and that place of rest. I have learned that even when I am at rest, it's not always easy, but there is a flow to it.

We still have to work at it, but there is an ease or a grace.

When I am out of my purpose, I am just hitting brick wall after brick wall and fighting more than I am resting.

The new formula for resilience is resting, and I want to get back to the original design and purpose for me.

Knowing your whys will also help you find a place of rest in which to do what you need to do.

**The map you choose will be up to you.
And your destination will depend
on your goals, wants and desires.**

Because I love you, I am going to let you in on my personal "whys" of approaching cancer as I did.

1. I want to live without fear of disease or death
2. I never want to be faced with cancer again
3. I want to live a healthy and active lifestyle for my family
4. I want to set the example for my family to pass on to the next generation
5. I want to keep my hair
6. I want to get up each day feeling good and rested
7. I want to fulfill the plan God has for my life

These helped me tremendously when I was lying in bed sick as a dog after getting IV drips to remove the toxins from my body and I felt like I wanted to die. I would remember that I wanted to keep my hair and be around for my grandchildren. It kept me from submitting to that hopeless feeling that was begging me to agree with it.

I remember Dr. Ben Lerner, one of my favorite mentors, telling me while I was going through natural cancer treatment, "No matter how determined we are, we will get tired, and when we know our "whys", our "hows" are very doable."

Knowing our "whys" is like giving ourselves a pep talk.

Maybe, for you, it's not overcoming cancer. Maybe it's going back to school when it is not convenient or easy. When I went back to school to study physical therapy, I wanted to be stable. I wanted to do something I loved. I wanted to provide for my children. Those were my "whys."

You were created with resilience. You were created to overcome. But the wrong mindset will hold you back.

You determine what you can accomplish (or not) by how you think.

When you say, "I can accomplish _____," you have to believe it because you were born to be resilient.

Even in Business

Resilience isn't just about physical health or emotional well-being, it affects every area of life, including business. I love what Martin Swilling had to say about resilience in *Forbes Magazine*:

> You can't survive as an entrepreneur without resilience, because you are going to fail at least once, maybe multiple times. That's the nature of trying something that's never been

done before. Resilience means not giving up, and being energized by what you have learned. As Thomas Edison said, "I have not failed. I have just found ten thousand ways that won't work."

If you need more evidence that great entrepreneurs survived through resilience, just look into the backgrounds of more recent entrepreneurs like Steve Jobs, Bill Gates, and Elon Musk. They all experienced multiple setbacks along the way, but they persevered to become some of the most well known and respected entrepreneurs of our time.[7]

Finding your "why" doesn't have to be a process where you chase your tail endlessly trying to discover what your life is all about.

Rather, it's an open door invitation to step into the passions of your heart.

And it's totally worth it.

▶

1-2 it's up to you!

Resilient Thought:

When you understand your "why", you are creating vision, purpose and passion toward your end goals. You are also giving yourself permission to say "yes" to the right things and "no" to the things that are not taking you in your desired direction.

1) What are things that based on your "why", you need to say "YES" to right now?

2) What are things that based on your "why", you need to say "NO" to right now?

A Resilient Person Knows They Must Own It

How to Take Accountability for Your Life ▶

Layne left his boss' office angry and disappointed. For the third consecutive year, Layne had failed to qualify for a promotion. As he sat steaming in his desk chair, Layne began to mutter under his breath all the reasons he felt like his supervisor was wrong. "The industry is suffering, so we should expect declines in sales." "It's not my fault that our team didn't finish the Atlanta project on time." "If we had better training, we'd have better results as a company." As the rapid thoughts of frustration raced through his mind, he began to think about how he was going to tell his wife, Jenni. "She doesn't understand me anyway. She thinks that I'm always focused on other things besides she and the kids." Layne's thoughts and inner-dialogue continued for the next few minutes, as he recounted the different areas of relational letdown in his life.

Chapter 3

▼

There is a vast difference between accountability, condemnation, and victimization.

Accountability says *I see my part*.

Condemnation says *I can't believe I did that. I'm such an idiot.*

Victimization says *I couldn't help it*.

The goal here is to learn to take accountability for yourself.

You are worthy of having control over yourself.

You are worthy of love.

And you are worthy of being taken care of, but this isn't someone else's responsibility, it is your own.

I understand the need for love.

All my life I was looking for love from men and I was changing every part of myself to feel pretty enough to get one. I got some, I actually got a lot, but I never got the love I was truly looking for.

From the time I was a preteen, I wanted attention from guys. That is probably why I stayed when I knew I should have left.

I remember the night very clearly. A friend and I were over at a house carrying on with a group of guys in our neighborhood. As my friend got up to leave, I said, "Oh I am good. I am going to hang here." And that was my first mistake.

I won't take the blame for what happened to me that night, staying behind or not, I didn't deserve to be gang-raped by six different guys.

There are no ifs, ands, or buts about it, what they did was horrifically wrong.

And as I stood in the front yard of that same house over three decades later, I had a choice to make: I could stay bitter and angry, or I could forgive them and move on.

It was my choice. It is always a choice to stay a victim or to overcome and move forward.

Resilience is about moving forward in the face of adversity.

But here's one of the most important things I could ever tell you:

Even in situations that are beyond our control, where we have been wronged, abused, cheated on, or any other type of painful life scenario, we have to accept that while we may have been a victim of the circumstance, we still have a part to play in bringing health and healing to our lives.

In other words, we are accountable for our own healing and wholeness, whether we directly caused the problem or not.

I had things done to me as a child which weren't my fault. I was misled and deceived and led into things that were just flat-out wrong.

But as part of my healing process, I discovered that taking accountability for the bad things in my life wasn't about ignoring what had happened, nor was it saying that I had to openly accept the people who had caused me pain.

Not at all.

It was about accepting that my future would have never been full of life, freedom, and fruitfulness if I had chosen to remain in a position of victimization. Holding onto a victim mindset will only make a person more bitter and dysfunctional in their relational interactions.

What Now?

Accountability is not about saying, "I can't believe this happened to me. Everything bad always happens to me. I will never be ok." That is the voice of a helpless victim that has no hope. And there is no such thing as no hope because hope is a choice, and frankly, hope is a Person, Jesus Christ.

> **It was my choice. It is always a choice
> to stay a victim or
> to overcome and move forward.**

Accountability says, "I see what happened to me, and while I may not like it, I choose to forgive myself and forgive those who hurt me."

Why?

Because I want to live a fruitful life and I can only move on and heal if I forgive the wrongs done to me.

My part was to face the reality of what happened, process the pain of it, and forgive so I could move on.

Blame will only lead us into greater despair.

It was my own distorted desire of coveting the attention of men which set into motion my decision not to leave that night. And then that particular night set into motion decades of drama from opening myself up to a place where I was trapped in the sex industry for over ten years.

In my life, I wanted more than anything to be accepted and loved. I just didn't know the healthy way to ask for it.

Instead, I found that always being sick seemed to get me the attention that I so longed for, which felt a lot like the real thing.

I started to experience severe pain in my reproductive organs. I talked about it incessantly. I would say to myself and others, "I am probably going to die of something to do with my female organs. I know I am going to die because of this."

I wanted attention, so I would think about being sick; I would imagine myself in a hospital bed so that someone would love me. I was always going to the doctor. It was in my head and coming out of my mouth, "I am going to die from some female issue." I would say it so that someone would feel sorry for me.

My words began to be my thoughts and my thoughts began to be what I believed, and I wanted everyone else to believe it too.

Over 20 Years Later

About a month after I was diagnosed with cervical cancer, the Lord brought me back to those memories where I kept saying that I was going to die from a disease of the reproductive system and now there I sat with a year to live.

It was sobering to say the least.

He then brought a scripture to my mind, Proverbs 18:21, that says, *"Death and life are in the power of the tongue..."*

And I heard His kind, loving whisper say to me, "Words have power, Andrea, and you have not been speaking life over yourself."

Stunned, I quickly got on my knees and *repented* of the way I was thinking.

Repentance isn't a horrible thing – it's simply stating that we are not in alignment with what God says about us, and it's embracing the truth in our thinking that He has a better plan for us.

In the original language of the Bible, to "repent" means "to change your mind," or to "change the way you think."

And if you change the way you think, it will change the way you live.

Repentance is a form of taking accountability for ourselves.

You don't take accountability for yourself if you can't see that you are believing incorrectly in any particular area.

It doesn't mean it's "all your fault" because that is condemnation. But it also doesn't mean it's all someone else's fault because that is victimization.

Obviously we aren't in control of what happens to us in life, but we are in control of our response to what happens to us in life.

This world is not how it should be and that's because God gave us free will, and we have all sinned and fallen short of the glory (or perfection) of God.

One of the fruits (or benefits of having the Holy Spirit of God living in us) is that we have self-control. Although we can't control the world around us as much as we might think or want, we can control ourselves.

We can control the choices we make and choices we often get to make are:

Will I stay a victim?

Will I beat myself up with condemnation? Or...

Will I take accountability for my part, forgive myself and those around me, and move on?

Choice is up to me, and it's up to you. You can own what your future looks like regardless of your past.

We start now.

We are co-laboring with something whether we mean to or not. We are either partnering with what the world tells us or we are partnering with God. Partnering with God often looks like partnering with His Word, the Bible. There are promises inside for all who believe in Him—promises that we can hold onto, that we can use to renew our mind back to its original design.

Promises like:

"For nothing will be impossible with God." Luke 1:37

"Cease striving and know that I am God." Psalm 46:10

"And do not be conformed to this world, but be transformed by the renewing of your mind, so that you may prove what the will of God is, that which is good and acceptable and perfect." Romans 12:2

These are just a few, but the last one is powerful because it is saying we can be transformed, we can change, we can be brought back to our original design by the renewing of our mind.

Renewing our mind with what He thinks about us.

I love that Bill Johnson often says how he can't afford to have a thought in his head about himself that God doesn't have about him.

Because if we are not transforming, we are conforming.

Taking accountability starts with being honest with ourselves and with God. He can help us be honest with ourselves and He is glad to help us; He created us and knows everything anyway, He is just waiting for us to ask.

> **Choice is up to me, and it's up to you.**
> **You can own what your future looks like**
> **regardless of your past.**

As we are honest with ourselves and where we are in life, we can then begin to decide who we want to be or who we want to partner with and there begins the renewing and transforming process.

*"My son, give attention to my words; Incline your ear to my sayings. Do not let them depart from your sight; Keep them in the midst of your heart. For they **are** life to those who find them And health to all their flesh."* Proverbs 4:20-22 [emphasis mine]

In this scripture, He is talking about His Word and saying His Word will give life to our minds, hearts, bodies, and souls.

This is what we can choose to partner with, but just like taking accountability, it is up to us to believe these words or not. We get to choose.

As we partner with the promises of God, we are able to come into a place of rest because we finally realize that we are not doing it on our own.

When we take accountability for ourselves, our actions, and our place in life, we can then see where we need to partner with God first.

We must avoid shame at all costs. Shame says that "something is wrong with me." But that is not true; even if we have done something bad, it's not *who* we are.

When we partner with the Word of God, He removes all shame and starts to transform us with the renewing of our mind.

The free gift of forgiveness comes from Jesus, so even if we did something we now see as wrong, maybe we made a wrong choice or a wrong decision or a mistake or we caused another pain, we can be set free and restored and come into right thinking with the Word of God, with the Person of Jesus Christ.

> **We must avoid shame at all costs.**
> **Shame says that "something is wrong with me."**
> **But that is not true; even if we have done something**
> **bad, it's not *who* we are.**

We will gain authority and come into a place of rest when we take accountability for ourselves because our viewpoint changes from one of no power to one that knows we have the power to change. And we don't have to do it alone. There is a way out, a way to a solution, a way to change the circumstance or turn it around.

> **When we take accountability for ourselves, our actions, and our place in life, we can then see where we need to partner with God first.**

Learning that I spoke death over myself from a place of deep, unmet need, then having to repent, was me taking accountability for myself. I didn't beat myself up or think *why me?* Well, actually I did at first but soon realized that was thinking like a victim and I wanted to be an overcomer instead.

I chose to repent and forgive myself and ask God for forgiveness. I did this by diving into God's Word. I did this by speaking the promises of God over myself. I was able to take accountability for where I was and reverse the lies that I had sown into my whole life. Now life was flowing in me because I was speaking life and not death.

I was not partnering with death anymore. The unmet need that was feeding that dysfunction was cut off by the transformation of my mind about my true identity as a child of God and what was promised to me because of it.

Resilience, in essence, all points back to the true source who made us that way to begin with, God.

If we are led by a false identity that brings on shame and condemnation, we are never going to take accountability because we are never going to want to face an identity that tells us there is something wrong with us because we believe it and agree with it to be true.

But that is not true.

If we partner with the promises of God, we partner with life. Then we can move forward, and moving forward isn't just part of being resilient, it is being resilient.

In an article written by Denise Foley for *NBC*, she talked about one of the most important traits that resilient people share:

They don't see themselves as victims whose fate is in the hands of others. "It's easy to blame other people for your problems and wait until they fix them," says psychiatrist Steven Wolin, MD, coauthor with Sybil Wolin, PhD, of *The Resilient Self: How Survivors of Troubled Families Rise Above Adversity*. "But then you never get to rise to the occasion and witness your own strength. If you think of yourself as a problem solver, life goes very differently.[8]

> **If we partner with the promises of God,
> we partner with life. Then we can
> move forward, and moving forward isn't just part
> of being resilient, it is being resilient.**

When you take accountability, you have authority, which opens your future opportunity.

▶

1-2 it's up to you!

Resilient Thought:
You will gain authority and come into a place of rest when you take accountability for yourself. It's because your viewpoint changes from one of no power to one that knows you have the power to change and/or move on.

1) What areas do you need to take accountability in? (Not blame, but accountability)

2) What areas specifically have you felt shame or regret about?

A Resilient Person Knows They Must LOL

How to Learn to Laugh

"When it rains, it pours," Susan thought to herself, as she picked up the various items that had just spilled out of her purse across the restaurant floor. This was seemingly the last straw for her emotions. Although the spill was quickly resolved, it capped off a week of ongoing bad news for Susan. Her best friend was diagnosed with a rare disease. Her husband found out he was on a short-list for possible layoffs, and her son was not doing well in school. Even though she couldn't control all the outcomes, she continued to internalize her problems and just wanted to stop and cry. From her perspective and rigid upbringing, "taking problems seriously" was the only solution.

Chapter 4

▼

It's been said by psychologists, the Bible, and even survivors of the holocaust that laughter can help heal our soul, change our mood, and shift the atmosphere around us.

According to Alex Lickerman, M.D., who wrote on laughter for *Psychology Today*:

> When faced with adversity, some people exhibit a great ability for turning to laughter as a soothing balm, while others remain less able to do so. While this may be a result of differences in upbringing or genetics, I often wonder if it's equally as much a matter of intent. Perhaps many of us simply don't think to try to laugh, either because we're too overwhelmed by suffering or because we think laughter in the face of suffering is inappropriate.[9]

A matter of intent.

Intent meaning to purpose or aim to do something.

It's not natural to laugh in the face of adversity, that's why it takes intent.

Understanding this key might have been one of the most therapeutic parts of my entire healing process.

Laughter is the Best Medicine

Studies show that laughter releases endorphins, which are your body's natural feel-good chemicals. And studies out of Korea have found that laughter has an effect similar to antidepressants.[10]

Who knew? I guess laughter is a form of medicine.

The thought that laughing in the face of adversity could be inappropriate at times is, of course accurate, but the more significant truth is that laughter can be used as a powerful weapon when faced with suffering.

Learning to Laugh

After the breakup with my ex-boyfriend, the one I ran to after my divorce, my daughter and I were sitting in the car with nowhere to go, and I thought, *We can do this. If we need to, we can just lock ourselves in here for a while until God shows us what's next.*

Before the thought even fully landed, the phone rang, and a very unlikely person on the other end said, "Andrea, I talked to my parents and they said you could live with them."

I say "unlikely person" because we often think it will be someone we know well who will help us in our time of deepest need. But what I have found it is often the least likely person.

The kind people who offered to take in my children and me were actually the parents of my now ex-boyfriend's ex-wife.

Dave and Debbie not only took us in as nearly total strangers, but they also housed us for a little over two years. They listened to me cry and talk and cry and talk about the same things over and over and over again. As I would cry and sob and talk about my disaster of a life, Debbie, the mother of the house, would listen with care and concern, and then out of nowhere, she would crack a joke.

> **Understanding this key might have been one of the most therapeutic parts of my entire healing process.**

And that joke was the perfect tension breaker.

It was as if she was poking a hole right in the middle of my drama. It would cut the tightness of my pain like a smooth-edged paring knife cuts through a delicious pumpkin pie.

Safe People

Debbie was what I would call a safe person. She was caring and loving, and I knew her jokes were not to harm me but rather to help me. We would be in the middle of one of my meltdowns and she would subtly say something that would send us into hysterics.

After laughing for a bit, it was like I forgot about what I was crying about earlier. She had a way of dropping humor into the situation that would break the intensity of my mind swirl.

It was a true gift.

When I think about my intense healing over those two-plus years, I remember back to moments of breakthrough that I had while starting to see the humor in my situation, the humor in myself. For the first time I was able to laugh at myself, and I can't tell you how much more fun that was then crying all the time.

God is not playing some crazy game with us when He's encouraging us to find joy in the midst of hard times.

It's actually quite the opposite.

When we choose joy in the midst of difficult times, it actually serves as a weapon to defeat Satan's influence in our lives.

Scripture says it this way: *"The joy of the LORD is your strength!"*

That means that when joy is a part of your life, it strengthens and equips you to live above the circumstances you may have experienced or are going through right now.

Let's make it practical. Think of a time when you experienced the most joy.

> **God is not playing some crazy game with us when He's encouraging us to find joy in the midst of hard times.**

Pause and remember how you felt. Joy isn't just a feeling, but the feeling of joy is definitely a big part.

Joy, according to Scripture, is a fruit of the Spirit.

Let's pause for a moment. I want to explain. You might be wondering what a "fruit of the Spirit" means, and I totally get it. If you think of fruit growing on a tree, you know that certain trees were made to produce certain kinds of fruit. I would say that fruit of the Spirit is somewhat similar. The Holy Spirit of God lives inside us, He holds the DNA of certain fruits or what we would refer to as attributes or characteristics.

The Bible teaches that the Holy Spirit is a Person. He is never to be referred to as "it." He is a mighty Person, the Holy Spirit of God, the living Spirit of God Himself.

The Bible also teaches us that the Spirit of God produces the fruit of the Spirit. *"But the fruit of the Spirit is love, joy, peace, patience, kindness, goodness, faithfulness, gentleness, self-control..."* (Galatians 5:22-23).

We get the suffering part, that is probably why you are reading this book. But did you see JOY as a fruit of the Spirit?

Exciting, huh?!

The Bible also says, *"...the kingdom of God is ... righteousness and peace and joy..."* (Romans 14:17).

According to Matthew 3:2, *"the kingdom of heaven is at hand."*

So, that means joy is at hand, and if it is at hand, doesn't that mean we can reach for it?

In Matthew 3, the Bible says we need to repent. Repent, if you remember, means to "change the way we think."

Right after it talks about repenting it says we want to do this because *"the Kingdom of God is at hand"* (Mark 1:15).

I wonder if joy is tied to letting go of mistakes, mess ups, and wrong mindsets? By giving them to the only One who can truly forgive us, we are set free into more joy than we think possible.

What we know is that joy, laughter, and happiness are helpful in life. Right?

Happiness is not needing anything from anyone, meaning you are so filled with the joy of God, with the love of God, with the acceptance of God, with the affirmation of God that you truly don't need anything from anyone else. That doesn't mean you don't have people around you, it just means you are going into those relationships already full, not needing anything to fill a deep well in your soul.

Debbie helped me to learn to laugh at myself in my most pitiful states, and it not only helped, but it also took my mind and focus off my issues and brought me joy.

Learn to Turn a Negative into a Positive

I was on a ministry trip to Phoenix and arrived very late. As I reached the hotel I was dead tired, exhausted, and thrilled to jump into my jammies and go to bed. As I opened my suitcase I found shampoo all over my clothes.

Great, what am I going to wear tomorrow? my worried mind asked me. But in that very moment, I knew I had a choice. I could either freak out and let my emotions run the show, or I could just laugh.

It was a choice.

I had to choose to reach for that fruit of joy that was ripe for the picking. I had to see the humor in the situation and in that moment choose joy.

Learn to Laugh at Wrong Thinking

Our thoughts are where every action begins. Steve Backlund wrote a brilliant little book called *Let's Just Laugh at That* which illustrates the point.

One of the lies they tackle is foundational to this entire chapter. It is the lie that says, "It's not my personality to be joyful or to laugh much." If you have ever thought this about yourself, you might be assuming some or all of the following:

- Joy is an optional fruit of the Spirit and is only for certain personalities.
- The Bible was speaking only metaphorically when it said that a merry heart is good medicine.
- Just as some don't have the right personality to be a loving person, I don't have the personality to be a joyful person.
- God regrets giving man a sense of humor.
- I cannot be joyful until my circumstances change.

These are what I would call lies. They are thoughts you believe that just aren't true.

The Truth: We all can, and need to, walk in abundant joy and laughter.

According to scripture, this is the truth of who you are and who God is.

- "The joy of the Lord is truly our strength,"

(Nehemiah 8:10).

- Laughter improves our health (Proverbs 17:22). Many scientific studies confirm that a merry heart is indeed good like medicine. (See my book Possessing Joy for insight on this.)
- As we become more like Jesus, we will experience more joy. "These things I have spoken to you, that My joy may remain in you, and that your joy may be full" (John 15:11).
- "In [God's] presence is fullness of joy" (Psalm 16:11). We may not always be fully joyful in God's presence; but if we never are, we might not be in His presence as much as we think. I don't write this to bring guilt but to help increase our expectation of joy manifesting as we pursue God.[12]

For more on overcoming lies with laughter, grab Steve's book *Let's Just Laugh at That.*

Back to the Basement

Debbie, the mother of that sweet family who helped me in my darkest season, knew that I needed to laugh, she knew the Lord and she knew His character was full of joy. And she was sneaky about it. When I was in the worst mood, bawling my eyes out, she would say something seemingly off the cuff and witty and I would crack up.

It would break the pain, even for a moment, and that was a gift.

She would always say, "Well, I am here for the comedy and the entertainment." It was amazing because her way of taking my pity and turning it into laughter was one of the main healing agents of my heart.

> **I wonder if joy is tied to letting go**
> **of mistakes, mess ups, and wrong mindsets?**
> **By giving them to the only One**
> **who can truly forgive us, we are set free**
> **into more joy than we think possible.**

And she was safe, and I knew there was no condemnation or shame.

A Few Practical Tips

Find people to be around that bring you joy, that you enjoy being around, that are fun and funny.

Don't watch sad movies.

Turn on a happy song.

My friend was told to watch funny movies after she was diagnosed with postpartum depression by a doctor.

It can be that simple.

Made in God's Image

I came to realize that I do love life. Even in the hardest times, I have seen the good. It wasn't my personality to be so intense, it was just what I was stuck in because of the lies I believed about myself.

I now know I love to laugh and I love my strong-willed personality, and those can be synonymous.

The pain we carry from childhood into adulthood can really block this sense of joy, this underlying love of our Father—a gift of His very nature that He gave to us. As life brings trials, we build walls to protect ourselves from more pain because it all seems too unbearable.

But that is the lie. If we process our pain and literally hand it over to Jesus, He will take it and give us joy for our mourning. It says so in Scripture, isn't that amazing?

Joy is part of our identity as a child of God. We don't often hear about that part of God, do we? But it's true.

A Good Question

Who are you going to allow to control your joy?

If it's the people and problems from your past or present circumstances, then I can almost promise you that you'll struggle to live above your circumstances.

It's your choice. And it's one that will determine the future path and trajectory of your life.

▶

1-2 it's up to you!

Resilient Thought:

Happiness and joy come from not needing anything from anyone, meaning you are so filled with the joy of God, with the love of God, with the acceptance of God, with the affirmation of God that you truly don't need anything from anyone else.

1) What areas of your life have you depended on people or position in order to try and find joy?

2) What are some previously painful circumstances that you are willing to stop and laugh about, knowing that you don't have to be defined by the pain?

A Resilient Person Knows They Must Face Their Fears

How to Transition Out of Your Comfort Zone ▶

Real Life Scenario

David slipped the five stones into his satchel and began to walk back to where his fellow soldiers were standing. For over six weeks the army had basically stood still as they were bombarded by ongoing threats of destruction and terror. David had just joined the frontlines of battle and realized very quickly that something wasn't right. As he listened to the accusations lobbied against he and his fellow friends and countrymen, he determined that there was only one thing that would bring victory. He had to face Goliath head-on.

Chapter 5

▼

When fear hits, we have two choices.

One, we can see it for what it is, call it out as a lie, and kick it in the face. Or...

Two, we can get stuck in the middle of the mind swirl. What if we "what if?" ourselves to death meaning "what if this happens?", "what if that happens?" as fear takes our entire being hostage.

I know, it sounds a little dramatic, but the truth is, fear will take you out and you must not allow it.

How do we see fear for what it is? We must pay attention to the thoughts in our head.

Socrates said, "The unexamined life is not worth living."

Yet few people sit down to weigh seriously that which controls their decisions.

When I began to evaluate my own life, I surprisingly found that fear was my uninvited tour guide in certain situations. I realized it was very important to know why I was running in the direction I was running.

Unfortunately, there are areas of our lives where we run in the complete opposite direction that we want to go. Or worse yet, we try to run towards our goal but with our heads turned around focused on the past.

As you might imagine, it is impossible to run very fast or in a straight line when your head is turned around looking behind you. That's why the Bible says that *we must forget those things which are behind us and reach for those things ahead.*

> ## How do we see fear for what it is?
> ## We must pay attention to
> ## the thoughts in our head.

Fear takes the past and makes a case for what will probably happen in the future. It is baiting you to turn around in order to get you off track.

It's Time To Take Inventory

What is it that you can't let go of?

What is it that you cannot forget?

What are those things that are keeping you from moving forward in life?

What is it that you fear?

The reason I ask is because you can't defeat your enemies until you know who they are.

Cancer was an obvious enemy. As soon as I heard the words come out of the doctor's mouth, fear showed up. And I know most of you would give me a pass and say, "Andrea that is normal to be afraid in that situation." I understand and appreciate your empathy, but according to the Bible, there is no reason to fear.

Why?

Well, I once heard it said that fear stands for:

F-alse

E-vidence

A-ppearing

R-eal

And the truth is, God knows fear is going to try to trip us up. This became a powerful thought to me.

That's when I had to make a decision. Who was I going to listen to? Fear or faith?

As you know by now, my faith is in the God who wrote the Bible. And He has promises that I can hold onto.

"Do not fear, do not be afraid, for I am with you." - God

I believe with all my being that He created the universe, and therefore, if there is anyone to trust, it would be Him.

His Word is filled with promises—promises of His help in our time of need, promises of life and not death. I had to choose to look fear in the face and walk past it to my God who I knew had a solution.

> **Fear takes the past and makes a case for what will probably happen in the future. It is baiting you to turn around in order to get you off track.**

Your faith may be in something different than mine, but in these times of fear or faith, you need to know who you have your faith in.

Fear That Hides

When you get a deadly diagnosis, fear is more obvious, but the anxiety I feel when I have to get on an airplane is harder to see. It's harder to detect the root of fear hiding behind my anxiety.

In my life, there was the moment I thought my daughter and I would have to live in our car. That brought fear, but thankfully and by the grace of God, I saw it rather quickly and was able to push it aside to do what had to be done.

Fear can seem understandable, but it's never God's will. Fear is often so ingrained in our way of thinking and culture that it feels like part of our personality.

But that's the furthest thing from the truth.

In each moment, we have to make a conscious decision. Will I allow fear to control me, or will I remind fear that I am in control, and more than that, God is in control?

Fear is a bully and it doesn't let up in the face of adversity. If anything, fear takes a seat at our table during challenges to see if it can win our agreement.

"Resiliency is born from your discovery
of strength within yourself to overcome."
– Unknown

Self-Defense

I loved teaching self-defense to people of all ages and have for many years. One of the things I've learned is that women don't have the same natural instinct to run into fear as men do.

I've always started class by asking those in attendance a question, "Are you capable of doing anything it takes to stay alive, and I mean anything?"

It's not about a right or wrong answer, believe it or not, but before they get into a life or death situation, they must ask themselves the question, would they be capable?

We, of course, train women to get away, but there are times you have to know who you are and what you are willing to do to stay alive or keep your family alive.

You don't want to wait until that moment to try to figure it out.

I do an exercise to help my class with this question. I ask them to close their eyes and imagine for a moment that they are standing in the backyard of their house and then hear a noise. As they walk into their home, they see an intruder has broken in with a weapon in hand.

"What are you going to do? For instance, would you be able protect yourself?" I ask.

While most people came up with their answers quite quickly, this one lovely lady whom I would have expected to say "yes, without a doubt!" said "I have no idea" and literally crumbled to her knees. She was so struck with fear that she couldn't even move.

Fear will physically, mentally, and spiritually paralyze you if you don't figure out how to overcome it.

That's Why We Must Face Fear

Facing your fears helps you to develop resilience. Once you face one fear and realize it is not strong enough to hold you back, you begin to realize you can face the next fear and the next fear and the next fear. You build up confidence that these fears are unable to hold you back.

> ***"Life doesn't get easier or more forgiving; we get stronger and more resilient."***
> – Steve Maraboli, *Life, the Truth, and Being Free*

In an article for *Entreprenuer.com*, Matthew Toren writes:

Resilience comes from facing your fears. You become better than your surroundings and transform yourself above the fear and into bigger and bigger success. Resilience starts with you, and it begins in your mind. Face your fears and learn to rise to face whatever is in front of you.[13]

There's the Bible story of a young shepherd named David who ended up in battle with his countrymen fighting an army who had a 9-foot tall giant named Goliath standing on the front-line challenging David and his fellow soldiers to come fight him.

David had such confidence that God would deliver him that, in the face of all fear, charged directly at Goliath – and killed the giant.

It might be one of the greatest underdog stories of all time, but the reason God put it in the Bible (you can read more about David in 1 Samuel 17) is to let us know that if it worked for David, it would work for us.

Simply put, face your "fearful giants" head-on and you won't be disappointed!

Facing your fears helps you to develop resilience. Once you face one fear and realize it is not strong enough...You build up confidence that these fears are unable to hold you back.

Noam Shpancer, Ph.D. writes about overcoming fear in for *Psychology Today*:

> ...confronting your fear instead of backing down brings about a sense of accomplishment and empowerment. Every time you confront your fear you gain power while your anxiety loses strength (I can tolerate it; it's difficult but not impossible; it's not the end of the world). Every time you confront your fear you accumulate evidence of your ability to cope (I did it yesterday; I can do it again today).[14]

When I was diagnosed with cancer, I asked God, "Why me? Why now?"

I heard Him whisper back, "Why not you? Why not now? You can overcome this Andrea, you are courageous, you are able to look fear in the face and do what you need to do. I have seen you do it before."

Cancer was never my enemy. Fear was!

After being told I had a year to live, fear of dying came knocking at my door.

I knew I needed to overcome fear first in order to overcome the actual disease.

I learned that courage was not the absence of fear, it was looking fear in the face and doing it anyway. Or as Kris Vallotton says, "Courage is fear that has said its prayers."

> **I knew I needed to overcome fear first in order to overcome the actual disease.**

It actually feels good to face fear and tell it "no, not this time." You feel accomplished, you feel stronger than you thought, and it drives you to overcome the next fear by saying, "I see you, fear, but I also see my God and I will not be afraid."

The Pool of Bethesda

In John 5, it states that many *"...who were sick, blind, lame, and withered, [[c]waiting for the moving of the waters; for an angel of the Lord went down at certain seasons into the pool and stirred up the water; whoever then first, after the stirring up of the water, stepped in was made well from whatever disease with which he was afflicted.] A man was there who had been [d]ill for thirty-eight years."*

Believe me, I am all for laying poolside; I am a California sun-loving, pool-bathing girl, but 38 years?

John goes onto say, *"When Jesus saw him lying there, and knew that he had already been a long time in that condition, He said to him "Do you wish to get well?" The sick man answered Him, "Sir, I have no man to put me into the pool when the water is stirred up, but while I am coming, another steps down before me"* John 5:5-7.

Note: Did you see that victim mentality there? His situation was real and understandable, but he was blaming others for the fact that he wasn't able to be well.

It is what came next that brought divine revelation and insight to me. *"Jesus said to him, 'Get up, pick up your pallet and walk.' Immediately the man became well, and picked up his pallet* (notice Jesus didn't pick it up for him or carry it) *and* began *to walk"* John 5:8-9 [additional thought mine].

Cancer was never my enemy. Fear was!

It wasn't about how he spent the 38 years laying by the pool; it wasn't even about those who got in before him or how he didn't have anyone to help him until Jesus came along. Rather, it was about being healed that day and moving on, step by step going forward, knowing who his Healer was and not fearing the future.

What's Fear Got to Do with It?

This is similar to the trust and expectation of our God. We must know Him, and we must often look fear in the face, pick up our mat and walk.

There are times that our distress, discouragement, and fear will become such a crippling part of our lives and our self-identity that we have difficulty moving forward.

So, you have to ask yourself, what issue, painful experience, or fear have you been hanging onto, or what fear has attached to you like a cancerous growth that needs to be removed and healed today?

Transitioning out of Your Comfort Zone

"Resilience doesn't just come from negative experience. You can build your resilience by putting yourself in challenging situations."
– Tara Parker-Pope, "How to Build Resilience in Midlife"

Although I loved Taekwondo, there were times I would put myself in challenging situations. Back then I couldn't say I knew I was doing it to face my fears, but boy was I ever.

I will never forget years ago, as I started sparring competitively and found myself at what they called the "bloodiest competition in the state of Missouri," which earned its name from the very relaxed way they went about the rules. Let's just say the sparring wasn't always fair.

I remember the girl that I was about to spar just so happened to be a professional kickboxer who was now trying her hand at Taekwondo. I sat there watching her kick the daylights out of this other girl while her coach yelled obscenities at me like, "See what she just did to her? It is going to be much worse for you."

I wanted nothing more than to throw up and run as fast as I could out of that place. Away from what was about to happen to me.

I was terrified.

My head and my body were not in agreement. As much as my mind said "get out of here as fast as you can," my body wouldn't move.

It was this resolve that didn't make sense at the time, but I stayed, and as I went out ready to spar, I took one step toward her and she kicked me so hard in my solar plexus (mid-section) that I flew into the next ring—literally flew.

My mind was telling my body "see, I told you this wasn't a good idea."

As I made my way back into the ring to set up for the next round, I was bloody, but I was not beaten.

She kicked me again the exact same way, a front kick to my solar plexus. I flew back over the very same platform into the next ring.

I guess I didn't learn. Or maybe I was ready to face my Goliath.

After I laid there for a minute rehearsing what her coach had said to me, something changed, and I got up. This time I was mad. I stood to my feet and said, "NO! You will not take me out, you will not have the final say." Something was raging in me. I got back up into position and did something different this time because the first two times I did the same thing and it got me knocked into another ring.

I went in as if I were going to move toward her but I flinched. She came forward to me and I was able to turn and back-kick her into the next ring, maybe not as dramatically as she kicked me, but I ended up winning.

She came up to me later and said, "I have never respected anybody like I respect you. The fact that you just stayed there blew me away. I learned something very valuable today that not everyone succumbs to fear."

> **But if we "stay" in the fight, we won't only win, we will realize just how strong we are meant to be in the first place.**

This story reminds me of life and our fight with fear. We may be terrified, and we may get kicked down a few times or knocked into another ring, but we must resolve to get back up and go at it again.

In other words, even if you lose a battle, you don't have to lose the war.

Fear will come at us with words like her coach said to me, words to intimidate us, which is what Goliath was using to intimidate David and his army.

But if we "stay" in the fight, we won't only win, we will realize just how strong we are meant to be in the first place.

And this is resilience.

The Truth Is...

Faith and fear cannot reside in the same heart. God did not give us a spirit of fear but of power, love and a sound mind.

Since we see in scripture the fact that having the Spirit of Fear is the opposite of having a sound mind, I would suggest that fear begins in the mind.

The enemy of our soul is called "the Father of Lies" by Jesus in Scripture, and since God says in His Word at least 365 different times not to fear, that's basically at least once per day as a reminder.

Fear is a liar.

In 1 Peter 5:8, Peter says, *"Be of sober spirit, be on the alert. Your adversary, the devil, prowls around like a roaring lion, seeking someone to devour."*

In the Greek language (the original language of the New Testament), the word sober-minded is a verb meaning to exercise self-control. We have to choose to not listen to fear. It is our choice, and we have to use our self-control in order to do so.

Are you wondering where to start? God's Word is the perfect place. I would suggest committing the following verse to memory because this is said by the Creator of the Universe.

"'Do not fear, for I am with you; Do not anxiously look about you, for I am your God. I will strengthen you, surely I will help you, Surely I will uphold you with My righteous right hand.'" Isaiah 41:10

God says not to fear because He is with us. He says He will strengthen us and help us; He will uphold us with His righteous right hand.

This is reassuring that we don't have to do it alone or muster up the strength on our own.

Scripture also says in 2 Corinthians 12:9-11 that *His grace is sufficient and that He is strong in our weakness.*

This is such good news.

Why?

Because we don't have to dig into ourselves to find strength, rather we can lean back onto God and find His strength. We can rest while we discover our resilient selves.

We were made for this; we were made to overcome fear; we were made to be held by our Heavenly Father.

Does this mean we still have to face our fears? Yes, but not alone, rather with the King of Kings and Lord of Lords by our side.

> **We were made for this; we were made to overcome fear; we were made to be held by our Heavenly Father.**

Even Science

In my research, I found an article about emotional resilience written by Eric Barker. In it he writes:

> Neuroscience says there's only one real way to deal with fear: you need to face it, head on. This is what the most resilient people do.
>
> When we avoid scary things we become more scared. When you face your fears they become less frightening.
>
> From Resilience: The Science of Mastering Life's Greatest Challenges:

> *To extinguish a fear-conditioned memory, one must be exposed to the fear-inducing stimulus in a safe environment, and this exposure needs to last long enough for the brain to form a new memory which conveys that the fear-conditioned stimulus is no longer dangerous in the present environment. Brain imaging findings suggest that extinction may involve a strengthening of the capacity of the PFC to inhibit amygdala-based fear responses (Phelps et al., 2004). Several approaches to treating anxiety disorders such as PTSD and phobias have been shown to be effective in promoting extinction. In essence, these therapies encourage the patient to confront the fear and anxiety head on.*

What do Special Forces soldiers think when facing the most terrifying situations? "I'm scared, but I can learn from this," or "This is a test that's going to make me stronger."[15]

"Fear points its sword to the place you were created for greatness."
– Jonathan Helser, Singer-Songwriter

This isn't a time for you to shrink back. Rather, it's a time for you to realize that with God's help, you really can face any obstacle or opposition in front of you.

Remember, overcoming issues in your life isn't about willpower or about pulling up your boot-straps and making things happen on your own.

It's about embracing God's unquentiable desire to show up on your behalf and empower you to do things that might otherwise seem impossible

It's time to embrace His strength, and face your battle.

▶

1-2 it's up to you!

Resilient Thought:
Faith and fear cannot reside in the same heart. God did not give you a spirit of fear but of power, love and a sound mind. This practically means that where you are experiencing fear, God wants to give you courage and strength to face it.

1) What areas have caused you fear in recent times?

2) What can you do right now to change your approach in dealing with your life battles?

A Resilient Person Doesn't Mind Having Their Butt Kicked

How to Embrace Your Training Ground ▶

Real Life Scenario

"Just three more times," Allen grunted as he continued his training up the steep hill. For the past hour and a half, he had been doing what he did five other days a week — preparing his body for his upcoming triathlon. Although Allen's extreme height made it such that he would probably never be fast enough to win the race, he didn't care. For his entire life, Allen had overcome things that would disqualify him in the eyes of others: a speech impediment, being adopted out of a foster home at age two and having to deal with the realities of losing a parent when he was just in grade school. Through it all, Allen graduated at the top of his class and built a successful company alongside his wife of over 20 years. Early on, Allen discovered that going through hard times, although never an easy thing to do, actually made him into a better man.

Chapter 6

▼

Resilience means facing life's difficulties with courage, hope and purpose, and refusing to give up. It is the quality of character that allows a person or group of people to rebound from misfortune, hardships, and trauma.

Resilience is rooted in tenacity of spirit, a will to embrace all that makes life worth living even in the face of overwhelming odds. When we have a clear sense of identity and purpose, we are more resilient because we can hold fast to the vision of a better future that God has for us.

> *"Resilience is the ability to work with adversity in such a way that one comes through it unharmed or even better for the experience."*
> – Unknown

I repeat the different definitions of resilience throughout this book because I want you to remember that this is who you were created to be. I want you to know that everyone faces difficulties.

I want you to remember you were not only created to survive this life, but you were intentionally created to thrive.

It's called the training ground. And it's the place where you decide what your future is going to look like.

You were created to move through this broken world and gain strength and strategy along the way.

I know it hurts. I know.

But we must not get stuck in the pain. We must move through to the beautiful part because that is what the training ground is all about. It is finding strength in the struggle. It is about partnering with God to find a way out and a way onward.

From the age of 12-36, I was physically, sexually, emotionally, verbally, and mentally abused. I was abandoned by my father in my late teens, I was 100 pounds overweight by the time I was 17, at 18-years-old I became a stripper and was trapped in the sex industry for over a decade. I had an eating disorder, I had two miscarriages before I was married, I was divorced after 18 years of marriage. I suffered from depression and constant thoughts of suicide, not to mention crippling anxiety. And to top it all off, at age 42 I was diagnosed with a deadly form of cancer and told I had less than a year to live.

My life was filled with brokenness and struggle—things done to me and things I did to myself and, unfortunately, to others.

When I say we better be ready to get our butts kicked, I am not talking about getting in the ring (like I did) and getting beat up more than we already have been in life. Rather, I am talking about a way of training to prepare us for this fight of life. Not to just survive, but to live in the promised abundance that our Lord and Savior promised us.

Jesus promised us abundant life. Let's go after it, even if it doesn't seem easy.

I am not one to give the devil much credit, but we are in a war, and although we fight from a place of rest and victory, we must fight, and in order to fight, we must train.

An Unlikely Tutor

I love the physical and emotional challenge that martial arts have brought into my life. I have had the privilege of incredible faith-filled instructors help me along the way to grow in my love for discipline, challenge, and Jesus Christ Himself.

I remember my first Taekwondo competition. I was a green belt, and had my sights set on the daunted task of becoming a Black Belt. I had only been training six months, and I was competing in a sparring match with another competitor.

I placed 2nd and I wasn't happy about it.

With my head sunk into my chest, I sat on the bench sulking about the fact I didn't win. I had to realize that beating myself up wasn't going to help. I realized years later that I learned more coming in 2nd than I did when I came in 1st.

Part of my training ground was understanding that I could actually learn from defeat and the negative things that had happened to me.

> **I am not one to give the devil much credit,
> but we are in a war, and although
> we fight from a place of rest and victory,
> we must fight, and in order to fight, we must train.**

You don't have to like it.

You don't have to enjoy it.

But, if you want to become everything you were created to be, you have to embrace it!

No matter what motivates you, if you want something to change, you have to take a step toward it. And … you have to be willing to get over the initial hurdles or perceptions from your past that would keep you from becoming great or moving forward.

God's Strategy and War Plan

In order to understand how to fight, we must first know a little bit about our opponent. In this life, we have an enemy named Satan. We see him depicted on TV shows from the 80's as a little creature in a red outfit on our shoulder telling us to do the "bad thing," which isn't far from the truth.

But the deeper truth is that He actually has a plan of attack against our life, it is failed of course, but he still has a plan to discourage, distract, and attempt to take us out with our own thoughts and actions, and the thoughts and actions of others.

And just like on an airplane where they teach you to put your own oxygen mask on first, you must deal with your thoughts and actions first before helping others.

But God … He always has a plan bigger and better than ours, and a way out too. He gives us a really awesome example in His Word that is easy to understand because He compares His protection over us to the armor a soldier would wear.

In Ephesians 6, we are told about the *armor* God has given to us to be able to stand against our enemy: truth, righteousness, peace, faith and the Word of God.

It is made for our protection because God provides all we need.

If we don't stay aware of the battle (aware, not obsessed), there is a big difference, the enemy can wreak havoc in our mind, which will wreak havoc in our body and our spirit as well.

> **We must move through to the beautiful part because that is what the training ground is all about.**

God has not only given us spiritual armor, He has also given us insight into our enemy. He has given us a strategy and a war plan to counteract what the enemy is trying to do.

Thank you God.

The Enemy's Strategy and God's Way Out

The darts the enemy tries to fire at us are things that might sound common to you. God knows they are things that will beat the enemy if we are willing to let go of them. Will you consider asking yourself and God if there are areas of "Letting Go" that you need to give to Him as I walk you through them?

Letting Go of Unforgiveness: If the enemy can convince you to refuse to forgive someone in your life who has hurt or even devastated you, he is winning. Forgiveness doesn't look like being in relationship with that person ever again, but it does look like letting them off the hook you have them on in your mind. It is releasing them. Much like I did three decades later as I stood in the front yard of the house in which I was raped, I didn't ever talk to those men again, but I stood there at that house and forgave them from my heart to God's ear. God is often the only one who needs to know you have forgiven although it is not bad to tell a friend so they can help you remember if the enemy tries to lie to you and tell you that you didn't forgive. Forgiveness is a choice, not a feeling.

Letting Go of Resentment: You have to be willing to let go of resentment, which is what is usually behind unforgiveness. In my case, resentment said, "you raped me and that caused me to hate myself and so I'll figure out unhealthy ways to prove that I can be loved." It can look like blaming that person who hurt you for the resulting sin in your life. Even though what they did was horrific, letting go of the resentment will be most healing to your life. The Bible actually says that resentment will rot your bones. It's so unhealthy for us, but if the enemy could keep us there he would like nothing more because his sole purpose is to take us out.

Letting Go of Retaliation/Revenge: You must be willing to let go of wanting revenge. I know it is so hard, but remember, all of these things sound like they will get us what we want, but they won't. They will only further hurt us as our hearts will harden and we will become even more broken. We can actually continue the cycle of pain in which we were injured if we don't let this go as well.

Let me pause and say, "I know without a doubt this hurts. I know because I went through this process myself, and as I write this book, I am praying for all of you to have the grace you need to let go—to find the peace that is promised in letting go. We are kicking the enemy in the face when we let go, and it's so important to realize that the enemy is ultimately the source of our trials, discouragement and defeat. (Ephesians 6:12)

Isn't that interesting?

Let's continue.

Letting Go of Anger: We must let go of anger because it is a harmful emotion if kept too long; it is ok to be angry, but it's not ok to let anger live in you. Be angry; tell God about your anger. He wants to hear it. He wants to help you through it. Suppressing anger won't help, being honest about it will. And once you have done this, you must give it over to God. If the anger pops up again, it's ok to go through the same process until it's gone.

Letting Go of Hatred: Hatred won't help either. It will keep your heart hard andyou will miss out on so much goodness and love in your life. It must be processed and given to the Lord.

Letting Go of Murder: I'm not specifically referring to physically killing someone. I'm talking about "murdering" your destiny or the destiny of others with the words that come out of your mouth. Murder with the mouth means speaking death over yourself, over others, or about God, and we must stop. It doesn't mean we suppress the negative feelings you have towards someone. You are allowed and should talk to God (or a professional who can truly help you through your pain) about what hurts you deeply, but once you have, you must consider laying it at His cross—meaning laying it down like He did His life for us and letting it go.

So, ask the question: "Who do I need to release, forgive and let go of as it relates to my life?"

You Have Overcome!

If you were able to ask yourself or God who you need to release in this last section, give yourself a high-five, a pat on the back, or a big smile because you just defeated the enemy in your life!

Amazing work!

If you weren't able to at this moment, be encouraged, put a marker in this section of the book, and come back to it when you are ready.

God is so kind and patient and He wants to process with you. You can even ask Him how and He will show you. Keep your eyes open. You might be surprised what He does.

> **By the Word of God transforming and renewing my mind, I have been able to live a life of courage, hope, and purpose, and so can you.**

I am so thankful for ministries like Pathway to Wholeness who taught me a lot of these concepts.

How He Showed Me How to Do It

I speak all over the country, and many women ask me, "How did you overcome all the adversity in your life? We know you say it was Jesus, but how? We want to know the details of how you got from Point A to Point B."

I struggled with this question for a very long time. I really thought I had made it clear that Jesus did it all.

Then it hit me again! My life verse—the verse that brought me back to life: *"And do not be conformed to this world, but be transformed by the renewing of your mind, so that you may prove what the will of God is, that which is good and acceptable and perfect."* (Romans 12:2).

He renewed my mind.

I went from a defeated, victim mindset to a mindset where I believed that I was an overcomer. After all, we are more than overcomers through Christ Jesus (Romans 8:37).

By the Word of God transforming and renewing my mind, I have been able to live a life of courage, hope, and purpose, and so can you.

Training in the Basement

The basement at Dave and Debbie's house was a similar training ground to the Taekwondo studio, but instead of training for a black belt in martial arts, I was training for a black belt in life.

As I laid there each night crying myself to sleep, muscles of resilience were being built, layers of pain and trauma were being shed off, and the real me was finally able to emerge, tear after tear.

The chaos that consumed my soul was intense, but the training ground was filled with so much peace and stability. It was a perfect place for my soul to work out the pain inside—to learn to let go and surrender.

> **There is a place for you to learn and it may look very different than you think. But embrace the learning; it will set you up for things to come.**

The basement was the most stable, peaceful place to learn. It was fully capable of handling the chaos that wanted to consume me.

You are often building character in the training ground of life, be it in the physical realm of Taekwondo or the spiritual and emotional realm of the basement.

There is a place for you to learn and it may look very different than you think. But embrace the learning; it will set you up for things to come.

We all have strengths and weaknesses. Weaknesses might not even be real weaknesses per sé, but they may be stemming from something deeper. This is why we must let the layers fall. We can't control how others treat us, but as resilient people, we can take what happens to us and allow it to strengthen and change us for the positive.

In your training ground, you learn courage, and you build strength and character. Because if you want to change and grow and be the best that God has created you to be, something is going to have to change.

Overcoming Your Obstacle

It generally takes an intentional mind shift and some self-will to overcome your obstacle.

We must go from an "I can't…" to an "I will…" attitude because "I will" shows determination; it is a powerful choice made by a very powerful person: you.

I am not just talking about the major traumas in life, I am also talking about the everyday struggles, like anxiety. I have suffered from anxiety for much of my life, and I remember thinking, *Why can't I just be normal like everyone else? Why do I have to suffer from anxiety? Why can't I just be normal?*

But instead of taking on that victim mentality and believing the lie that something was wrong with me, I determined not to carry it as my identity and ask God for His strategy to beat it.

If we ask, He will indeed give it to us. It may be simple things like memorizing scripture or taking a supplement that helps keep you calm in times of anxiety or listening to a song that helps you sleep. The strategy doesn't have to be elaborate. Honestly, it's usually pretty practical. Our God is a practical God. He is simple and straightforward, we sometimes want to complicate Him, but that isn't often His way.

> **Instead of taking on that victim mentality and believing the lie that something was wrong with me, I determined not to carry it as my identity and ask God for His strategy to beat it.**

What's the Goal?

The goal is to overcome and move forward. Overcome what?

That's up to you. It can be anything from a wrong mindset, to a lie, to a past hurt, daily anxiety, trauma from the past, depression, illness, relational hardship, unforgiveness, bitterness, all of the enemy's tactics mentioned earlier, or feelings of hopelessness or unworthiness. These are all things that we can overcome with God. We can bounce back and be resilient. It's in our DNA; it's who we are already.

Whatever it is for you, you must press on toward the goal.

The Greek word (meaning the original language in which the New Testament of the Bible was written) for "press" is the verb "dioko" (long o sounds), which means to "put to flight, pursue, pursuing (continuous), run after, seek after."

When Paul (in the Bible) talks about "pressing on" to take hold of that which has taken hold of me, he is talking about a position of posture. That position requires courage, hope, and resilience.

Paul refers to our life as a race, or as I like to call it, the journey!

Three Motivators for Your Future Success

Really, just three words:
Courage.
Hope.
Purpose.
Here's what I mean.

Courage is the ability to do something that you know is difficult or dangerous. Courage is persevering, having mental strength. Courage withstands danger, fear, or difficulty.

Hope is an expectation and desire for good things to happen.

Purpose is having a target that you keep your focus on.

The Christian walk can be likened to that of an athlete's way of life. Even if you don't consider yourself to be athletic, it's important to realize that athletes know that being the best doesn't happen overnight or come by chance; it comes through determination and dedication: studying the game, training daily for hours on end, and learning from one's mistakes when competing.

The Christian walk is like an 'athlete's journey' where we strengthen our spiritual muscles by immersing ourselves in the Word, by following God's guidance for life ('the rules'), by not being distracted by the world and by keeping our eyes on the goal, Jesus, so that when it comes to competition time (the trials of life), we are better equipped to deal with struggles and can come out as winners (literally wearing the 'victor's crown').

Thank God for the redeeming power of Jesus Christ that works in us through the Holy Spirit! Through Him and by Him, we are being conformed to His image so that, like the Apostle Paul, we can say with confidence, *"I can do all this through Him who strengthens me"* (Philippians 4:13).

And as one of my favorite pastors, Chris Hill, says, "Never trust a warrior who doesn't have any battle scars."

Jesus is a good one to trust because His battle scars were intentionally taken just for you.

▶

1-2 it's up to you!

Resilient Thought:
It generally takes an intentional mind shift and some self-will to overcome your obstacle. You must go from an "I can't..." to an "I will..." attitude because "I will" shows determination; it is a powerful choice made by a very powerful person: you.

1) What areas have you resisted learning or growing, whether it was too hard or too uncomfortable?

2) What are some empowering goals you can set in areas that you know you need to grow?

A Resilient Person Purposely Isn't a Loner

How to Have Life Giving Relationships ▶

Real Life Scenario

As Joanne walked back to her apartment on the other side of campus, she began to wonder why others seemed to be so good at relationships and she was not. After all, she had plenty of indicators throughout her life that she was smart, talented, and pretty, but in spite of those "accolades," she wasn't finding fulfillment in relationships. More disturbing was the reality that she had stopped trying to make new friends. Nobody understands me and the struggles I go through, she thought. But as she quietly moved up the stairs and slid her key into the door of her roommate-free living space, she began to realize that maybe she had been going about it all wrong. Maybe the tension she felt in establishing and maintaining relationships was a good thing.

Chapter 7

▼

As humans, we have all traveled distinct paths; we've all learned life lessons in very different ways. It's valuable to see situations and circumstances from diverse points of view. It's healthy to understand the triumphs and trials of others. It's not only encouraging to our own lives, but it also helps bring forth perspective and compassion for one another.

A group of people that want to learn, love, and do life with each other is called community. In a community people usually have a common interest or live in a similar area. A community of people is often built on a common characteristic or interest be it social, economic, political or faith-based.

You might be wondering what community has to do with becoming resilient.

The truth is, it has everything to do with it.

"Many studies show that the primary factor in resilience is having caring and supportive relationships within and outside the family. Relationships that create love and trust, provide role models and offer encouragement and reassurance, help bolster a person's resilience."[16]

In the book *Bowling Alone*, author Robert Putnam said the greatest social epidemic in American life is loneliness.

Loneliness is defined as sadness because one has no friends or company.

Putnam shows how we have become increasingly disconnected from family, friends, neighbors, and our democratic structures. … He draws on evidence from nearly 500,000 interviews over the last quarter century to show that we sign fewer petitions, belong to fewer organizations that meet, know our neighbors less, meet with friends less frequently, and even socialize with our families less often.[17]

We weren't created to be alone.

Why?

Well, for one, community is fun and fun brings laughter to our lives. And we know laughter is a big part of being resilient.

Are you having fun in life?

Do you have people to have fun with?

Community is also encouraging, and we all know that we need encouragement from others in different seasons in life.

I once heard if you want to know if someone needs encouragement just look to see if they are breathing! I can't remember who said it first, but that was profound for me. As we often think the people who seemingly "have it together" don't need encouragement when that is not true at all.

Pouring encouragement into one another is how we find courage. We absolutely need to learn how to encourage one another; at the same time, we must learn how to receive encouragement from those around us.

Proverbs 12:25 says, *"Anxiety in a man's heart weighs it down, but a good word makes it glad."*

A kind word is needed when anxiety hits, and anxiety hits when we don't see a solution or a way out and lose hope. Often when trials come in life, we need to know that there is a way out, and a kind word from another person can help.

Encouragement often sounds like a kind word to another person.

Let's face it, our world is filled with anxiety, but according to God's Word, *a kind word cheers up our heart*. We need to pay attention to our heart for it is the wellspring of life. Every word we speak is an outpouring of our heart.

If you are thinking, *Andrea, the people around me are negative*, I would say to you, "Try to be the opposite of what surrounds you and see if you can indeed affect your current community with life and positivity. Words bring life or words bring death. You can speak life or death over people.

If you find the people that you are surrounded with are infecting you more than you are affecting them, it may be time to find a different community. I'm not talking about "jumping ship" in relationships simply if someone is having a bad day; I'm talking about where the culture and attitude of your community are infecting you like a bad disease!

We weren't created to be alone.

You can't choose your family, but you can choose your community.

Community Attracts the Holy Spirit

The Bible says that the Holy Spirit is present whenever believers gather together. A great example of this was the gatherings of the people during the early church of Acts, who made a habit of meeting together, eating together, and worshiping together.

This is where the current church gets its mandate to create community because God knows that He formed us to thrive in relationship with others. Plus, the Holy Spirit is where the joy, peace, patience, goodness and kindness of the Lord are found. The Holy Spirit lives in every believer of Jesus Christ and is a free gift to those who choose to believe.

Community Reinforces Identity

Proverbs 13:20 says, *"He who walks with wise men will be wise, But the companion of fools will suffer harm."*

The great "prophet of old" Vanilla Ice put it like this, "Show me your friends and I will tell you who you are."

> **You won't find your destiny
> until you find your people.**

If you find your perspective to be negative all or most of the time, you may want to look for people that are positive and hang around them, learn from them, because you will become like those you surround yourself with.

My time studying martial arts showed me that while I could practice my forms in my living room and work hard alone, when I stepped into that studio with my like-minded Taekwondo family—where we had comradery—it would empower me in a distinct way. They built me up, pulled more out of me, and pushed me higher, and I would do the same for them. I have found that others can often see more in you than you can see in yourself.

Simply put, life is meant to be lived in relational community. It's what makes us better, even with all of the perceived messiness that can accompany it. Because, let's face it, we are all a hot-mess in progress.

It's this tension of doing life with others that actually causes us to rise above in life.

Your people are so important because they are tied to your purpose in life. It's been said that your destiny is tied to your relationships.

Kris Vallotton, a strong voice of our generation, says, "You won't find your destiny until you find your people."

I love this.

From psychologists to theologians to pop stars of the 80's and historians, they all agree that community and resilience are closely knit together.

Community: The Solution for Addiction?

Community is so crucial amidst humans that it is even said to be the major player in the recovery of addiction.

In an increasingly widely disseminated TED Talk titled *Everything You Think You Know About Addiction is Wrong,* British journalist Johann Hari discusses the available research into the underlying causes of addiction, and concludes, rather brilliantly, that the opposite of addiction is not sobriety, it's connection.[18]

Professor Peter Cohen says that bonding and forming connections is how we get our satisfaction. If we can't connect with each other, we will connect with anything we can find. He says, "we should stop talking about 'addiction' altogether, and instead call it 'bonding.' A heroin addict has bonded with heroin because she couldn't bond as fully with anything else."[19]

Canadian psychologist Bruce Alexander looked at the results of studies in which rats were placed in empty cages, alone, with two water bottles to choose from: one with pure water, the other with heroin-infused water. Those experiments showed that as time passed these rats would uniformly get hooked on and eventually overdose from heroin. The researchers unsurprisingly concluded that the potential of extreme pleasure, in and of itself, is addictive. Case closed, right?[20]

Not for Alexander. He was bothered by the fact that the cages in which the rats were isolated were small, with no potential for stimulation beyond the heroin. Alexander concluded that they all got high because they had nothing else to do. In response to this perceived shortcoming, Alexander created what we now call "the rat park," a cage approximately 200 times larger than the typical isolation cage with Hamster wheels and multi-colored balls to play with, plenty of tasty food to eat, and spaces for mating and raising litters. And he put not one rat but 20 rats (of both genders) into the cage. Then, and only then, did he mirror the old experiments, offering one bottle of pure water and one bottle of heroin water. And guess what? The rats ignored the heroin. They were much more interested in typical communal rat activities such as playing, fighting, eating, and mating. Essentially, with a little bit of social stimulation and connection, addiction disappeared. Heck, even rats who'd previously been isolated and sucking on the heroin water left it alone once they were introduced to the rat park.[21]

Perhaps that's why we are in trouble. We naturally look to our social networks for help whether they offer emotional support or simply a helping hand.

"Having friends you can talk to and share your concerns with, maybe having them help you get a perspective on things—that's where social ties can be useful," says resiliency researcher, Elliot Friedman.[22]

And Then ... Boundaries

Boundaries can be a helpful tool when it comes to community because if you say yes to a group of people or a few groups of people, be it your family, your church family, your work, or your friends, you will have to learn to say no to something else.

A favorite on this subject, Danny Silk, says "It's easy to think that it is important or even spiritual to offer all people unlimited access to our lives. But everyone who tries to do this eventually discovers that it is not sustainable, healthy, or spiritual ... at all."

It is important to know what we want to say yes to in life, mainly because that will help us determine our no.

Boundaries aren't about putting up weird walls to keep people out, it is more about keeping your yeses in front of you so you can keep saying yes.

As important as community is, it is not codependency.

Codependency is excessive emotional or psychological reliance on another.

With this new formula of resilience that you are considering, we said:

Rest (God Directed Activity)
+
A "Return" to the Original Design
=
Resilience.

Rest can mean different things to different people. For me, rest means relying on God, knowing that I am not God, knowing that it's not my responsibility to figure out everyone else, and it is also falling back into His arms and believing Him at His Word (which takes the pressure off my own ability to accomplish "said thing"), and allowing Him to direct me.

Relying too heavily on other people can bread unhealthy tendencies.

There's a fine line between being a loner and being codependent—neither are healthy. Henry Cloud, Ph.D. wrote in "The Simple Scoop on Boundaries":

God created us to be free, and to act responsibly with our freedom. He wanted us to be in control of ourselves. He was behind that idea all along. But we misused our freedom and as a result, lost it. And the big fruit of this loss of freedom was the loss of self-control. We have felt the results of that ever since in a wide variety of misery. Consider a few of the destructive alternatives to self-control:

- Controlling relationships where people try to control each other
- Faith that is practiced out of guilt and drudgery instead of freedom and love
- The replacement of love as a motivator with guilt, anger and fear instead
- The inability to stop evil in significant relationships and cultures
- The inability to gain control of our own behavior and solve problems in our lives
- The loss of control to addictive processes[23]

It's not about balance in life, it's about health in all areas of your life. What I mean is this: When we are always trying to "balance" things in our lives, it can actually keep us from dealing appropriately with a particular issue or life scenario that might actually require more of our time. As a parent, I discovered that while I wanted to balance the time and investment into each of my kids, there were simply seasons of life where one of them would require a significantly greater portion of my time and investment than the other.

In the end, it did "balance out," but when our mindset is to be as healthy as possible in our approach to our different relationships and responsibilities, we'll find greater fulfillment and greater fruit in our endeavors.

So...

Are you healthy in your relationships with others?

Are you healthy in your relationship with yourself, because that is very important?

Are you healthy in your relationship with God, if you have a relationship with God?

If you do see God as your first love, then you know very well you are commanded to love Him first with all your heart, soul, mind, and strength. We know how to love Him because He loved us first.

The Cathedral Tree

I heard one of my favorites, Jenn Johnson, talk about the way a particular redwood, called the cathedral tree, created community.

It was approximately 800 to 1000 years ago that a huge tree stood in the middle of a formation. When it fell, it didn't die.

The roots and burls of the stump sprouted, and nine trees happened to grow together in a circle around the original mother tree's stump, which has long since rotted away.

**It's not about balance in life,
it's about health in all areas of your life.**

This tree is not only the site of Easter services each year but also many, many weddings today. It serves as a place of celebration.

Psalm 133:1 (NIV) tells us, *"How good and pleasant it is when God's people live together in unity!"*

Here's the simple key to remember: Relationships are worth the effort. That's right; great relationships require effort. But the result of being committed to a community is a life that far exceeds anything you can ever dream.

▶

1-2 it's up to you!

Resilient Thought:

A group of people that want to learn, love, and do life with each other is called community. In a community people usually have a common interest or live in a similar area. It can take time to form one that is valuable to you, but it is completely vital for your long-term growth and success.

1) What has kept you from experiencing authentic community on a regular basis?

2) What changes are you willing to make in order to establish a healthy community of people around you (regardless of how radical it may seem)?

A Resilient Person Doesn't Always Have to Be the Smartest One in the Room

How to Be a Lifelong Learner ▶

Real Life Scenario

Nate brushed quietly past his fellow students in the long, narrow hallway that led to the cafeteria. Like he had done hundreds of times before, he opened his paper sack and began to arrange its contents on the table in front of him. As he was taking the first bite of his whole grain sandwich, a soft, familiar voice spoke up, "Nate, I was wondering. Would you be willing to spend a little time with me and help me figure out how to solve a problem from my calculus assignment?" said Julianna, a sweet, brown-eyed classmate who Nate found easy on the eyes. "Sure, I'd be happy to help you, but why me?" he asked. Julianna's response startled Nate, "Well, Nate, it's because whenever we answer questions in class, you don't pretend to know something that you really don't — it's like you understand when to speak up and when to be silent. And candidly, that's really refreshing, and so I know if I ask for your help, you'll only tell me the truth." A wide and embarrassing smile slowly grew across Nate's face that he felt probably looked like a clown face to his cute friend. "Sure, Julianna, show me what you've got, and if I understand where you got stuck, I'll see if I can help you figure it out." Nate realized that his insatiable passion for reading, learning, and developing might not such be such a bad thing after all.

Chapter 8

▼

If you are always the smartest person in the room, you aren't going to grow.

Obviously, this is a principle and not an absolute, but what's been a life-altering lesson for me to learn is that regardless of my position, status, or achievements in life (or even a lack thereof), my life will have an upward trajectory if I am continually open to learning and gleaning from others who have already been on the path you are currently on. And so will yours.

I remember meeting an older gentleman at the gym; he was so kind, wise and very book smart. He knew a lot about everything and had several degrees. But what I loved about him most was his humility.

He was the kind of guy that seemed so willing to impart his wisdom to me, almost like a father figure.

I was always caught off-guard when I would ask him a question and he would tell me he didn't know the answer. This was a little shocking to me because I never thought of wisdom in this way.

I thought if I were going to be a wise person I needed to know the answer to everything. This was probably because I never felt good enough. If I got an A, I was mad that I didn't get an A+.

I thought if I didn't know the answer to a question, there was really something wrong with me.

But that was a lie.

In all honesty, I would often make up answers to appear smart; I thought I had to know it all— if I didn't, I thought I was stupid.

But this man changed the way I thought. I knew he was wise and I saw in him an even deeper wisdom when he would admit to not knowing the answer to a question; that changed me.

It may sound small to you, but isn't it often the small things in life that can bring about the most change? I believe it is.

If we have our learning eyes and ears tuned into all circumstances and situations around us, we will find learning everywhere we turn.

Learning is wisdom. And wisdom is what we pass along to others to help them.

When I was fighting cancer, I knew I needed people around me who knew more than I did, people that were educated in this area, people that had walked this road before that from whom I could gain knowledge and wisdom.

After I won my battle, I got to write a book about how I overcame cancer and give it as a gift to anyone who needed hope for their journey. It brought me so much life to help others through what I had just been through.

I would say this is how God created us: to learn, and then pass things along.

That's why I believe God set up the world in families. If you think about it, we were all born into a family, some more functional than others, that's for sure. But still, we were all born into a 'community' of people that help us to learn things we don't know how to do.

Our parents had parents and that's how they learned. I know none of us had perfect parents, nor were we perfect parents ourselves, and if you don't have children yet, just know you won't be perfect either.

But there is always learning to be had from those who have done what we have not done before.

> **This is how God created us: to learn,**
> **and then pass things along.**

Even if it is how we don't want to do things, there is value in that as well. If we look for the value, we will find it.

God is intentional, so I know this was intentional on His part too.

If your family was dysfunctional like mine, God had a redemption plan and gave us yet another way to learn from one another. He said all those that come into His family are family to one another as He is our Father. God gave us a second family in case the brokenness of our original family was just too much to bare.

He is Our Provider

I remember when I came into God's family by receiving Jesus Christ as my Lord and Savior, He put people around me in church and in small group settings that literally resembled a new family. Were they perfect? Of course not. Did they replace my original family? Not at all.

They were just added to my life as a bonus and a very big blessing.

He wanted me to grow in Him, so He knew I needed some people that had done this "following Jesus" life before me. These different groups within my Christian walk helped me to grow, learn, overcome challenges, and become better at my pursuit of God and a better way of life.

We all need people who have walked ahead of us that will be there to lead us and guide us and help us along the way.

I wrote this book because I want to share with you what I have learned the hard way so that you might be able to learn it quicker and easier than I did. My hope is that you won't have to go through what I went through to learn what I have learned. But instead, you would stand on my shoulders and go from there.

If you feel you are too far gone, let me encourage you. You're not!

> **We all need people who have walked ahead of us that will be there to lead us and guide us and help us along the way.**

There's never been a story under heaven where the circumstances are so dire that God wasn't able to rewrite the ending of the story and redeem it.

I'm simply saying that learning from the mistakes and pitfalls of others can help you avoid the same mistakes and pitfalls.

Leadership

My husband is the owner and leader of his company—the boss man, you could say. He often says how hard it is for him to grow unless he is very intentional about finding others in different sectors of business to learn from. He needs people to teach, challenge, and support him in his growth process because a lot of his energy is focused on the growth of others.

The good news about him growing is that it always trickles down to those under him.

When at our best, we are often referred to as a river because a river is flowing at all times. The goal is to have resources (be it people or recorded material) pouring into us as we pour into others. A river is always flowing.

If you think about it, that's how a daughter, mother, and grandmother work together. Again, no family is perfect, but as a grandmother teaches a mother and a mother teaches her daughter, it seems like this was no mistake in how God, the Creator, planned the world to function.

You need people who have walked ahead of you in life to be there to lead and guide and help you, and in turn, you can help those behind you.

What we have to remember is that mentors aren't always hands-on. Our needs as humans are probably too vast to be met by one person even if we did have the most amazing parents, teachers, and mentors.

I see it more like a raindrop effect.

The Bucket Theory

Think of yourself like a bucket.

You have many "need to and want to" learning situations in life, but instead of a water fountain type of learning from just one person, you can learn many things from many people, like raindrops. These little bits of information coming into your bucket from many sources fill it to capacity and then watering others with that knowledge, you receive again, and water again, etc. It is a process that never has to stop.

Isn't it beautiful?

You may be fortunate to have one or two hands-on mentors in your life in different seasons, but God has used women and men I have never met in person, like Joyce Meyer, to lead me into powerful breakthrough—so don't overlook what might seem simple. That's called grace!

A Mixture from Heaven

Joyce was like a mother to me while I was in my season of healing in the basement. God also gave me Dave and Debbie who were there for me in tangible form, able to hug and talk to.

He knew that season was a particularly hard one, so He surrounded me with a mixture of resources and people to help me get free.

He does that; He knows just what we need.

Life works in seasons, and people come in and out of our lives in this same way, in seasons.

Wise counselors can also often come from the most unlikely places, like my friend Shawna, who was the ex-wife of my ex-boyfriend. Shawna taught me (through text messaging) the wisdom of God's Word. We can't count out modern day technology as one of God's tools; He will use it all.

> **Life works in seasons, and people come in and out of our lives in this same way, in seasons.**

Shawna, who was younger than me, became somewhat of a mentor to me for a season.

Mentoring: Three Kinds of Mentors

Up close and personal: for example, Dave and Debbie, who came alongside me in season where I needed hands-on mentoring.

Distant, but intimate: this can come from media, teaching, podcasts from a teacher who shares very intimately but isn't someone you meet in person.

Salt and Pepper: periodic sprinkles of wisdom that often come from random sources but definitely add flavor to your life.

Be Teachable

I learned from my martial arts instructor that the best way to benefit from mentors is to be teachable and coachable more than it is to have natural ability and raw talent.

This was surprising to me.

Isn't that exciting?

Practical Tips for Learning from Others

There is a leadership expert that a lot of people love named John Maxwell. He did an exercise that I thought would be valuable to include in this book. When he wanted to learn something new, he would make contact with the person he wanted to learn from and let them know he would pay them for their time. He always brought a legal pad to write down what he learned and a list of questions to ask. He was hungry to learn.

People love a hungry person that wants to learn, and without expectation, when John's time concluded with the person he was learning from, they would never accept his money. I would bet that it's because they appreciated the way he honored them.

1. Valuing and honoring someone is important;

whether you offer to buy them a meal or a coffee, you are showing them that you understand the value of their time.

2. Bringing a legal pad prepared with questions is another way to show value and honor. The goal is not to talk during these times but rather to listen. In John's case, it demonstrated to the prospective mentor that John had a willing heart to listen and learn.

Three questions to help you get started:

1. Share with the person what you admire about their gifting or their position, but then quickly turn it around and ask them about their path to getting there.
2. Ask them what they consider to be the single greatest mistake they felt they've made along the way so that you might learn from them.
3. Ask them what is one simple thing you could do in order to help you stay on a path that is similar to theirs.

These questions will prompt you toward other questions. And don't forget to come ready to learn and listen.

Resilience and Learning

In the *Harvard Business Review*, Rich Fernandez wrote about resilience:

While working as a director of learning and organization development at Google, eBay and J.P. Morgan Chase, and in my current work as co-founder of the learning solutions company Wisdom Labs, I've seen over and over again that the most resilient individuals and teams aren't the ones that don't fail, but rather the ones that fail, learn and thrive because of it. Being challenged — sometimes severely — is part of what activates resilience as a skill set.

More than five decades of research point to the fact that resilience is built by attitudes, behaviors and social supports that can be adopted and cultivated by anyone. Factors that lead to resilience include optimism; the ability to stay balanced and manage strong or difficult emotions; a sense of safety and a strong social support system. The good news is that because there is a concrete set of behaviors and skills associated with resilience, you can learn to be more resilient.[24]

We can't just wish, whine, and hope for a strong support system, we often have to be intentional to build one—not pulling too much on any one person but being open and honoring of those who may be placed around us in each season of life.

Have Resilient Role Models

Again, I go back to Eric Barker's article about emotional resilience:

When you study kids who grow up in impoverished circumstances but go on to live productive, healthy lives, what do you find?

They had great role models who provided a positive example and supported them.

From *Resilience: The Science of Mastering Life's Greatest Challenges*:

One of the first psychologists to study resilience, Emmy Werner, followed the lives of children who were raised in impoverished homes with an alcoholic, abusive, or mentally ill parent. Werner observed that resilient children – the ones who grew up to be productive, emotionally healthy adults – had at least one person in their lives who truly supported them and served as an admired role model (Werner, 1993; Werner & Smith, 1992). Our research has found a similar pattern: all of the resilient individuals we interviewed have role models whose beliefs, attitudes and behaviors inspire them.

But sometimes it's hard to find people we know we want to be like. That's okay. Southwick and Charney found that it's often enough to have bad role models — people who provide an example of what you don't want to be.

From *Resilience: The Science of Mastering Life's Greatest Challenges*:
Although we generally think of role models as providing positive examples to admire and emulate, in some cases a particular person may stand out in the opposite way – embodying

traits we emphatically do not want to have. We can think of such a person as a negative role model.[25]

I find it interesting that role models and wisdom can even come from what we want to avoid becoming like, but God is truly kind to use all circumstances to help us learn and grow if we so choose too.

> **Life works in seasons, and people come in and out of our lives in this same way, in seasons.**

A few tips when intentionally looking for people of wisdom to learn from:

1. Look for people who can support you, not carry you.
2. Look for people who build you up. We have talked a lot about those who you encourage and those who encourage you. Remember, sow what you need. If you say, "I don't have anyone who encourages me," maybe be the person you need and see how God gives it back to you. Keep your eyes open; it might not come from where you think.
3. Look for people that will push you through. I remember my basement days, crying for hours on end and complaining about my ex-boyfriend. I will never forget when Dave, the dad of the house, looked at me a nd said, "It must be hard living for two people Andrea."

When he said that I realized I was carrying problems t hat weren't mine to carry. His fatherly love in that moment pushed me past my insecurities.

4. Say no to the naysayers. You can be nice, but people can have other agendas that keep you from being you and fulfilling your destiny, dreams, and visions.

Even though we don't want to listen to naysayers, we do want to listen to wise counsel. The scripture is clear that *"Plans fail for lack of counsel, but with many advisers they succeed"* Proverbs 15:22.

And remember, these counselors shouldn't take the place of God. He is the head of these counselors, almost like the Senior Counselor if you will.

Leslie Crandall, a Bible teacher, uses an illustration called "safety sandwich" which is helpful. She says that the bread on top is you asking the Lord, the meat in the middle is you asking your wise counsel, and the bread on the bottom is you taking that wisdom back to the Lord.

This strategy will keep decisions safe and filled with wisdom.

Like any advisory board, fill your group with those you want to be like, do your homework, interview, pray, and ask God to place the right people into your team.

If you will keep yourself continually open to learning, growing, and developing, it actually will remove any ceilings or lids from your future.

The sky's the limit for you.

▶

1-2 it's up to you!

Resilient Thought:

You can't just wish, whine, and hope for a strong support system, you often have to be intentional to build one—not pulling too much on any one person but being open and honoring of those who may be placed around you in each season of life.

1) What areas do you want to grow in?

2) Who are the peole you can learn from, whether up-close or from some type of distant learning?

A Resilient Person Isn't a Very Good Narcissist

How to Be Self-Aware of Your Emotions, Reactions, and Persona ▶

Real Life Scenario

Angie knew something was wrong with her relationship with Jim, but she was struggling to put her finger on it. Jim's outer features were nothing short of amazing: tall, strong, outgoing, and incredibly intelligent. But after months of dating, Angie found herself "drained" after any kind of significant discussion with her handsome beau. Angie had some upbringing in church, and she remembered how her sweet grandmother would repeatedly tell her, "Honey, whenever you don't know what to do, ask God to help you figure it out." So, as Angie was preparing to go workout with Jim, she asked God to help her. After only a few minutes of working out together on the fitness machines that faced the large, bigger-than-life mirrors, Jim said out loud, "Wow! You look really good!" Angie blushed at the statement and thanked him for the compliment. "No, I was actually talking about myself." Angie now was fully clued-in to the problem.

Chapter 9

▼

The Bible talks a lot about loving your neighbor
as yourself.

That isn't always as easy as it sounds because most of us struggle to love ourselves.

Loving oneself is much different than being self-absorbed. Someone who is self-absorbed is called a narcissist, but there is a big difference between that and self-love.

> Psychologist Stephen Johnson writes that the narcissist is someone who has "buried his true self-expression in response to early injuries and replaced it with a highly developed, compensatory false self." This alternate persona to the real self often comes across as grandiose, "above others," self-absorbed, and highly conceited. In our individualistic and externally driven society, mild to severe forms of narcissism are not only pervasive but often encouraged.[2]

In other words, at the root of narcissism is said to be a deep pain and an even deeper sense of unworthiness.

Unworthiness can come from self-hatred.

Either way, when we are extremely focused on self, we lose the ability to focus on others. But at the same time, if we don't love ourselves, we will struggle to love others.

It's not exactly black and white. It is something we have to discover ourselves.

Love Without Narcissism

In our culture, we have all kinds of definitions for love. To some, love is a feeling, to others, it's an action, and to me, love is God because scripture says God is love.

If God is love and we are created in His image, we are the image of love.

It sounds simple and pretty, but is it?

If you live in a world where you think you are worthless, yet you try to cover it up and present a false-self like a narcissist does, trying to love others will be difficult because you are not in touch with your true self and therefore you will have no way of loving that true self.

What Does This Have to Do with Me?

If you are concerned that you may be a narcissist, the truth is you probably aren't.

There is this false humility in our culture that is just as damaging as narcissism that says "we must stay humble and please people."

We are called to be self-aware, but that does not mean editing how we want others to see our lives to the point that we are no longer effective in what we were created to do.

Since the opposite of narcissism can actually work against us, we must be aware of why we are acting and reacting the way we do. In our society of instant judgment, we are now guilty until proven innocent and it can cause us to live in a place where we self-edit our lives to such a degree that we don't step into who we were born to be.

> **If God is love and we are created in His image, we are the image of love.**

We become paralyzed by fear. None of us are perfect. But we must be honest and open and try to have a heart of humility and ask ourselves or the Lord, "Am I walking in the right direction?" It's actually a crime to not confidently step into who we are called to be and what we are called to do just because it may occasionally ruffle a few feathers.

Avoiding narcissism does not mean that you are constantly acquiescing to the opinions and perspective of others. It really just means you are sensitive and aware of other people's viewpoints and how your daily living can affect their lives.

The bottom line is, you have to be confident in what you were created to do. In my life, that looks like an ongoing, personal relationship with God through Jesus Christ. I believe He gives us not only our identity but also a call to accomplish in life.

If we stay connected to Him, we can find our true confidence in who He says we are instead of the opinions of others.

On more than one occasion, I have had to come back from relationship setbacks. I had to ask myself, "Am I going to let that set back define what God has for me because I am terrified I am going to offend somebody?"

It's a real question we often have to ask ourselves, and I have had to do that more than a few times.

But I've realized that a setback is just a setup for a powerful comeback.

Sorting Through the Issues

Thinking only of ourselves can cause tendencies toward narcissism or victim mentality. But ignoring yourself can also have adverse consequences. Neither of these is where we want to live. This is why we must understand self-love and then self-sacrifice.

Some of us know that we are children of the living and all-powerful God. The invitation to be a child of God is open to all, but not all accept it. This God is so powerful that He can call every person on earth His favorite because we are. He is a father that gives to His children richly, giving to one doesn't mean He can't give everything that is good to another as well.

If we stay connected to Him, we can find our true confidence in who He says we are instead of the opinions of others.

A scarcity mindset—or in a Christian context, you may hear it called the orphan spirit— tells us that "because they got that, there is not enough for me." This orphan spirit says God has a limited supply of good things. It is trying to tell you that once He gives to one, there won't be enough for another.

This simply is not true.

A person with narcissistic tendencies will use manipulation and guilt proclaiming, "I've given you so much, and you're so ungrateful," or, "I'm a victim and you must help me or you're not a good person." They hijack your emotions and convince you to make unreasonable sacrifices.

A resilient person, on the other hand, says:

1. "I am grateful because I see purpose, hope, and courage in everything I do or receive from others."
2. "I am not a victim. Instead of saying poor me, I will admit it hurts, but I know that I will overcome this too."

Getting Out of Your Head

When going through pain, it is helpful to get outside your head— not to deny the reality of your pain or situation, because grieving is very important, but to find perspective and turn off the mind swirl. Kimberly Yam wrote:

> Giving back has an effect on your body. Studies show that when people donated to charity, the mesolimbic system, the portion of the brain responsible for feelings of reward, was triggered. The brain also releases feel-good chemicals and spurs you to perform more kind acts — something psychologists call "helper's high."
> According to research from the University of Texas, "Volunteer work improves access to social and psychological resources, which are known to counter negative moods.[27]

We don't want to volunteer for selfish reasons but to volunteer for any reason is going to help you and help others. That's never a bad decision.

A Tendency Toward Narcissism

At *Psychologytoday.com*, Preston Ni, MSBA, wrote about narcissism:

> It is interesting that narcissism is often interpreted in popular culture as a person who's in love with him or herself. But it is more accurate to characterize the pathological narcissist as someone who's in love with *an idealized self-image*, which they project in order to avoid feeling (and being seen as) the real, disenfranchised, wounded self. Deep down, most pathological

narcissists feel like the "ugly duckling," even if they painfully don't want to admit it.[28]

The pain of life sometimes will take us down to a place where we can't function for a season, and in those times, it is ok to let the Father heal you. Seasons of healing where the focus is on you, is healthy, but you can't stay there, or it will become unhealthy.

Life, like the weather in most of middle America, happens in seasons. There is a time for everything, including a focus on healing, but taking a step outside of your comfort zone to help others will often be very helpful for you in putting one foot in front of the other. Otherwise, self-pity will have you wiping your tears and affirming that thought that says, *Poor me. Why me?* And trust me, I know how it goes; I lived there for a long time.

During my healing season and what I lovingly refer to as my training ground in the basement of Dave and Debbie's house, I found myself all alone one week with no one to bare my soul too, no one to make me laugh, and no one to take care of.

Dave and Debbie had gone to Germany, and my daughter was on a six-week trip.

What was I going to do with myself? I wondered.

One day, as I was praying for God to take all the junk and poison out of my soul, I screamed, "Jesus, hug me!"

I felt His embrace and then saw a picture in my mind's eye of a little three-year-old girl in a pink dress.

I sensed He was saying, "Andrea, if you want the pain to stop, you need to stop dwelling on it and rehearsing it over and over again."

I had endured six months of crying every single night. Could I just stop? I didn't know.

I was thinking, *How, God? How do I just stop?*

Then the thought popped into my head that at church they were asking for volunteers. I didn't want to do it, I could care less, I had only been there for two months, but I forced myself to go. I had nothing else to do, and this was something that didn't cost any money.

Here is the thing, you don't have to be excited about everything, you just have to be willing.

As I walked into the church dragging my issues like a backwoods-hike backpack, I suddenly felt such peace.

And to my utter surprise, I ended up having a lot of fun. I probably wasn't the most fun to be around, but I made some friends that night.

What I didn't know (but God did) was that I needed to walk into an environment that was the opposite of the environment inside me, which was pure and unbridled chaos.

I started to engage in conversation, meet new people, and get out of my head, and I felt lighter than I had in months. I no longer felt like a had a ton of heavy textbooks on my back.

I started to laugh for the first time in six months. I got outside of myself and became part of what was happening.

He knew I was going to have a good night, and it was the first time in six months I didn't cry myself to sleep.

I was engaging in my new reality and it was the most basic thing. Simple, yet profound. A couple of hours made a world of difference.

"Research ... has found that volunteerism (defined as two hours per week over many years) reduces mortality rates by 40 percent. This is really quite remarkable research. Since it isn't a randomized clinical trial we can't be exactly sure how this works but it may speak to the notion that serving others can be both good for your mental and physical <u>health</u>."[29]

In a study of psychological resilience among American military veterans, higher levels of gratitude, altruism, and a sense of purpose predicted resiliency.

What if We Could Really Care About Others?

Psychological altruism means acting out of concern for the well-being of others, without regard for your own self-interest.

It is argued that true altruism doesn't exist, that we are always looking for a way to meet our own needs even in helping others. I would say that can be true, but the Lord knows the needs of both sides. In my example, He knew the need of the church and He knew my need to get out of my own head, so He laid that on my heart to go, and bam!, it worked.

> **Seasons of healing where the focus is on you, is healthy, but you can't stay there, or it will become unhealthy.**

Did I know I was going to get my needs met? No, I didn't. Was it the main motive in my heart? No, it wasn't.

But did it help me? Yes! It did.

My goal is to help you find ways to rest in who you are and find a way out of what you are stuck in; helping others will be a way for you to love your neighbor as yourself.

Is volunteering true altruism? To be honest, I don't know, and I don't necessarily think it matters.

Tara Parker-Pope writes about helping others:

> Any way you can reach out and help other people is a way of moving outside of yourself, and this is an important way to enhance your own strength," said Dr. Southwick. "Part of resilience is taking responsibility for your life, and for creating a life that you consider meaningful and purposeful. It doesn't have to be a big mission — it could be your family. As long as what you're involved in has meaning to you, that can push you through all sorts of adversity.[30]

"You want your dreams to come true, embrace the dreams of others." Matthew Barnett.

That is the key to living your life 97% narcissistic free.

You and I were made to be living examples of God's beauty and love in this earth. Let's determine to express this in a way that inspires and attracts others.

▶

1-2 it's up to you!

Resilient Thought:

Thinking only of yourself can cause tendencies toward narcissism or victim mentality. But ignoring yourself can also have adverse consequences. Neither of these is where you want to live. This is why you must understand self-love and then self-sacrifice.

1) *In what areas have you neglected your own inner care that you need to build confidence in ?*

2) *With the highest level of self-awareness possible, what areas have you been overly "you-focused"?*

A Resilient Person Knows It's a Process

How Not to Give Up – Ever ▶

Real Life Scenario

*After what seemed like an eternity, Abigail had grown
tired with wrestling with her current environment. Just
a few weeks earlier, she was living an unencumbered life
— primarily devoted to eating, sleeping, and light doses of
physical activity. But then almost overnight, things started to
change around her, and the changes forced her into what was
now a very discomforting and almost paralyzing situation.
The intensity had actually made it difficult for Abigail to
have any clarity as to what others around her were doing.
Where had her friends gone? What would her future look
like? In the midst of the tension, and when she thought
she couldn't make it any longer, her breakthrough finally
happened. A door of opportunity opened in front of her,
and she realized that her discomfort had brought
metamorphic change. She opened her new set of wings,
left her cocoon, and flew away into a new life of adventure
as a beautiful butterfly.*

Chapter 10

▼

I think the word "process" may have gotten a bad rap.

The truth is there seems to be a process to just about everything in life.

There is a process to grow a garden, for getting food from a field, for getting food from animals, for raising children, and a process for losing weight, etc.

We may not call it all a process, but that is indeed what it is, and it's not bad, it's just the way the world works.

Do we get a pass on the process sometimes? I believe so. But do we get a pass on the process all of the time? No, we don't.

The struggle in our microwave generation is that we like things drive-thru style. We want them *now*.

I am not just talking about food, although that applies here too.

I am talking about the process of sowing and reaping. When I look back, I see how this principle has played out in my life; I just didn't know what to call it at the time.

Sowing can be done with words, food, wisdom, encouragement, finances or even thoughts. The principal itself crosses borders and works in just about all areas of life.

Dr. Charles Stanley, one of my favorite Bible teachers, says, "You reap what you sow, more than you sow, and later than you sow."

It's one of those quotes you have to read and sit with for a minute to fully take in.

I liken it to a rosemary plant. I can plant one rosemary seed, and it will grow and grow and grow one seed will produce a lot of rosemary. I reaped way more than I sowed.

> Dr. Stanley says, "The Lord gives principles in Scripture to serve as warnings and as an encouragement. In Galatians 6:7, His Word states, *"Do not be deceived, God is not mocked; for whatever a man sows, this he will also reap."* Every farmer understands the meaning of this principle."
>
> He continues, "The fact that we reap what we sow is good news for those who sow good habits, but a frightening thought for those currently involved in ungodly activities such as promiscuity, drug and alcohol abuse, neglect of family, or mistreatment of others in order to climb the ladder of success. We cannot sow crabgrass and expect to reap pineapples. We cannot sow disobedience to God and expect to reap His blessing. What we sow, we reap. Let us not deceive ourselves: We will reap the harvest of our lives."
>
> "This same principle is a comforting and reassuring thought to those who faithfully labor under difficult circumstances. "For whatever a man sows, this he will also reap." Faithfulness in such situations will produce a rich harvest in the future, for our heavenly Father always keeps His promises."[31]

The Process of Seed to Harvest

According to the National Coffee Association, there is a ten-step process that a seed must go through before it hits your cup in the morning.

Farmers take a field through a process somewhat like God takes us through life. The farmer will cultivate, irrigate, fertilize, and plow as part of his process or journey for his beloved field.

He wants that seed to grow into the flourishing stalk of corn it was always meant to be.

> **Do we get a pass on the process sometimes?**
> **I believe so. But do we get a pass on the process**
> **all of the time? No, we don't.**

In the same way, our Creator wants to help us grow into all we were meant to be.

In my experience, it is a very personal process specifically designed for each individual. We should be careful not to compare ourselves—each Child of God is in their own process. Scripture says that God knows every hair on our head and His thoughts of us outnumber the sand of the sea. I am from Southern California and grew up near the beach. Trust me; there is a lot of sand. He knows us very well.

I think one misconception about God is that He doesn't care about us, but that couldn't be further from the truth. He cares so much He can't stop thinking about us.

And this process He takes us through isn't punishment, if anything, it's the exact opposite. He wants to see us bloom into the beauty which He created.

His heart for us is to become all He created us to be, and the truth is that takes a process that often feels like a journey to an unknown destination.

The key here is to remember that there is gold all along the trail. There is always so much to learn on the journey and if we see it for the adventure that it is, we can and will find joy in it, which is what our Creator wants for us, joy.

Mining for Gold

I will never forget a field trip I went on as a kid where one of the activities was panning for gold. As we stood in a line at the large tin trough, we were excited because we just knew our pans full of dirt and soot just had to have some gold. We sifted it, swirled it and shook it around trying to discover the gold. It was a painstakingly slow process of removing all the dirt and allowing the gold to settle to the bottom.

As I was living in "the basement" for two years of my life, I realized God wanted me to see the gold He created in me. He was allowing all the dirt in my life to be shaken off, like bitterness I had towards my failed relationships, the false identity I received from men, harmful words I had spoken over myself and the negative things others had spoken over me, and my obsession with my appearance. I could go on, but He knew I needed a good swirling, sifting, and shaking to get to my gold.

Trust me, I didn't like this process at first, but as I look back, I see how necessary it was and how much of my true self was hidden under so much muck and mire.

> **Our Creator wants to help us grow
> into all we were meant to be.**

In these seasons of removing the dirt to discover the gold, it might be a more self-focused season. Sometimes it's so intense you don't have capacity for much else and that is ok. You definitely can't stay there, but for a season it is good to allow the Lord to work as intensely as He wants.

He processes different things at different points in our lives because He knows us best. It's up to us to submit to the process and allow the gold to come forth.

As painful as the "basement season" was, it was where I first learned what true love looked and felt like. I was 37 years old with two darling children, divorced, and had a boyfriend shortly after my divorce.

There was a place in my heart that was created for Love Himself, God. Until I found that, all the other "things in the world" would not give me the satisfaction that I needed.

The love I was looking for all my life was right in front of me. It came from a place I never suspected, but it was as real as anything I can imagine.

The Adventure of Process

Adventures aren't foolproof; they involve risk and some steep uphill climbs at times, but there are always lessons to learn along the way—lessons which will reap a harvest for a long time to come.

That is why I do what I do. I have been through my share of struggles and uphill, treacherous climbs, but I want to share what I have learned so that you may be able to bypass a few of those "cliffhangers."

> **His heart for us is to become all He created us to be, and the truth is that takes a process that often feels like a journey to an unknown destination.**

We have the best guide. The One who Created us wants to lead us through it all. In the planting and the harvesting, He will lead us to know what to plant and what to sow.

I remember a heartbreaking situation in my life where I feared losing a part of myself in a person that was so dear to me. I knew I had to let go when the Lord said, "Andrea, if you try to fix this, it will only be temporary, but if I fix it, it will be eternal."

It was over a two-year period that God led me in the way I should handle things with this person, and in the end, He was right. I can look back now at this relationship, which was ultimately reconciled, and I'm so grateful that God showed me how to restore it. Through that process, I learned when to sow and what to sow into this person. His timing and way were exactly what was needed. And I am so thankful.

Renewing Our Mind

Renewing our minds is a form of sowing healthy seeds into our lives. I would say it is one of the most important ways you can sow seed into your own life. It goes back to the Scripture I keep mentioning throughout this book, Romans 12:2, *"And do not be conformed to this world, but be transformed by the renewing of your mind, so that you may prove what the will of God is, that which is good and acceptable and perfect."*

A lot of us have either had or still have this misconception about God that He causes the hard things in our life, but I don't believe that at all; the brokenness of humanity is what causes the brokenness in our lives.

The world was given to us by a Creator who loves us most and wants to see us flourish and grow to be delicious and beautiful, just like a farmer would his crop or a gardener her vegetables.

He knows what kind of irrigating we need and what kind of organic fertilizer will help us blossom into our original design. God doesn't cause any of our pain, but He knows what we need to do to get to the other side of it.

Renewing our mind means changing the way we think. It's not just going through the motions, it is going through the process.

I remember when I was a weight loss coach and would see people make all the proper changes and see results. If they sowed the seeds of good decisions and habits, they would reap the harvest they so desired. But if they didn't allow their minds to be renewed, they would often come back having gained all their weight back plus some extra.

Why?

Because they didn't endure the process, they simply wanted a quick fix and forced themselves into the motions that yielded the outcome they were looking for, but it wasn't sustainable.

They didn't go through the process of renewing their mind, changing the way they thought about life.

Going through the motions might get you where you want to be, but if you haven't changed your mind along the way, you won't maintain it.

I remember being at my favorite juice bar when I was on a pretty intense liver cleanse. It brought me back to the days of juicing thirteen times a day when I had cancer. I remember the joy I felt at working on my healing even though I was going through something so horrific. Looking back years later, I see the joy in the midst of my suffering.

How could I see the joy in suffering, you ask? I believe it was because I was overcoming something people said I never could. I wasn't trying to prove anyone wrong, I was just so encouraged and filled with hope by the people God brought into my life to help me.

We can't always see the joy in the middle of our suffering, but when we look back, we can often see His blessings and His hand on a lot of the little things.

The process of overcoming cancer was hard and scary, but as I changed things, I began to feel better, and more importantly, I was getting well.

What Is It You Want?

"Delight yourself in the Lord; and He will give you the desires of your heart" Psalm 37:4. A friend of mine recently gave me an example that helped me to understand the meaning of 'our desires' a little better.

Let's say you want an island. Yes, an island; sounds crazy, just go with me here.

Let's pretend that is the desire of your heart—an island. It's what you want more than anything.

> **We can't always see the joy in the middle of our suffering, but when we look back, we can often see His blessings and His hand on a lot of the little things.**

But the process of getting it is not happening fast enough.

You don't know how to swim, but you aren't focused on that, you just know you want the island. God knows if you get your island and something happens, and you need to swim to safety, you aren't going to be able to, and this would not be good for you. You may not understand this and get upset at this fact.

The process of "teaching you how to swim" is so you will know how to deal with and handle things when they happen. If you aren't willing to go through the process as He leads, this blessing you so desire could be just the opposite, it could take you out.

I remember crying and crying because all I wanted to do was be in a relationship when I was in the basement.

Deep down, I knew I wasn't ready for it, but this didn't stop me from wanting it so badly.

God knew I needed to go through the process of being reconstructed. He needed to pull down the false identity of who I thought I was so He could bring to light who I really was.

Even if He had answered my unwise request to have a man right then, it more than likely would have ended up similar to a crash diet scenario. It would have worked for a little bit but then like most of my other relationships it would have ended in a mess.

Knowing what I know now, Joe, my amazing husband, wasn't ready either. We were both still in process.

God promises that we are going to have an abundant life.

But it comes with a process in order to see the promise fulfilled in our lives.

> **I know without a doubt that
> "The Promise"
> +
> "The Process"
> =
> "The Promotion."**

Once we step into that promotion, we want to be able to stay there.

All that pain was worth it. All those nights crying myself to sleep in the basement were worth it.

Why? Well, because God is a master at making something beautiful out of our pain and problems even when we cause them!

It was amazing how through the pain there was such beauty in it all. I just didn't realize it at the time.

And that's the beauty of your process—God has an ending for your story that can exceed your best expectations.

But if you want to see the beauty, it will require something of you—you need to give Him the ashes of your life.

It's totally worth it. I promise.

▶

1-2 it's up to you!

Resilient Thought:

The process of change is so you will know how to deal with and handle opportunities and challenges when they come your way (and they will come). If you aren't willing to go through the process then you are actually cheating yourself of long-term wisdom and blessings.

1) What areas are you recognizing that you are in the right kind of process right now?

2) What changes do you need to make to your perspective or approach in order to see healthy results from your process ?

A Resilient Person Knows They Must Let Go of Mistakes, Mindsets, and the Moronic Actions of Life

How to Choose Excellence Over Perfection ▶

Abraham stared into the night sky and breathed a soft sigh of relief. The events of the preceding months (and even years) flashed through his mind at a frantic pace. Defeat, failure, opposition, discouragement, relational strains, financial ruin – these were just a short list of some of the "issues" that had plagued his life. As he reflected on the intensity of his life, and more recently, the intensity of what he had just endured, a sense of gratitude began to come upon him. He realized that all of the perceived setbacks were really a divine setup for His comeback. After a few moments of enjoying the quiet breeze blowing against his bearded face, with a combination of humility and confidence running through his veins, Abraham Lincoln stepped back inside the White House to begin his tenure as the 16th President of the United States of America.

Chapter 11

▼

It's true. We all made mistakes in life whether it's been years or maybe as recent as an hour ago. It's the human condition to miss the mark. It's impossible not to.

But being able to let go is the goal. It may be the hardest and most powerful thing you will ever do.

Resilience is flexible. It's not rigid. It's able to sway back and forth. Resilience doesn't have a spirit of perfection anywhere near it.

To hold ourselves to a standard of never making a mistake is holding ourselves to a standard of perfection, which is not only impossible but will also make you miserable in the end.

I can honestly say that one of the biggest roadblocks that kept me from being a resilient person was my perfectionism.

Perfectionism will consistently cause you to feel like a failure because there is no such thing.

We were never made to be perfect; we were made to be excellent.

And there is a big difference between the two.

Excellence is a spirit in which you do something. It has more to do with the motivation and attitude in which you do something, rather than the end result.

Perfection is intolerance for anything that is not in perfect form.

Perfection starts inside you and eventually works its way out and around you, influencing people, places, and things with which you associate.

Excellence is doing whatever it is you do in such a way that it raises the standard without condemnation or judgment of others.

For example, I have a friend who I love and value very much, and she has become very wealthy over the past several years. It seems her level of expectation of others has gone up with her net worth. We were out to dinner a few years ago, and the level of perfection in which she held the wait staff and the restaurant seemed very unusual. Her inability to see any reason for flaws or mistakes was bordering on a level of perfectionism that I could tell wasn't making her happier.

And when you go about life this way, it ends up slowly eroding your ability to enjoy it. It also keeps you from having a clear perspective on what reality is because it seems that you're living below the line at all times. All of a sudden it takes "out of this world experiences" in order for you to find satisfaction in everyday life.

The pursuit of excellence will require hard work and a diligent attitude, but if done wisely, it will be pursued by God's strength not our own.

> **The pursuit of excellence will require hard work and a diligent attitude, but if done wisely, it will be pursued by God's strength not our own.**

A Fine Line Worth Pursuing

Perfectionists	Pursuers of Excellence
Focus on doing things perfectly.	Focus on the reason for the task, not on how it all appears.
Value themselves by what they do.	Value themselves by who they are.
Can be devastated by failure	Learn from failure
Want to be number one.	Can live without being the best, especially when they know they've given their best.
Live with a mindset which doesn't allow for mistakes.	Keep a focus on what matters.
Can often struggle to find peace of mind.	Live with a sense of peace that tomorrow is a new day.

Perfectionists will not complete things and procrastinate. They are terrified of making mistakes and find themselves stressed, anxious, and desperately focused on not failing.

I know this because I was a textbook perfectionist.

I had to decide who I was and what I was going after. I had to decide that I was a resilient person in pursuit of excellence and no longer partner with the lie that said I was a perfectionist.

Perfection does not bend. It's rigid. Perfection will keep you from your destiny. Perfection will keep you from fulfilling your

God-given potential and gifting. So, let's not mistake the mantle of excellence with the spirit of perfection.

The Message (MSG) translation of the Bible puts it like this in Romans 12:1-2, *"So here is what I want you to do, God helping you: Take your everyday, ordinary life-your sleeping, eating, going to work, and walking around life-and place it before God as an offering. Embracing what God does for you is the best thing you can do for him. Don't become so well-adjusted to your culture that you fit into it without even thinking. Instead, fix your attention on God. You'll be changed from the inside out. Readily recognize what he wants from you, and quickly respond to it."* It's important that you not misinterpret yourselves as people who are bringing this goodness to God. No, God brings it all to you. Pursue excellence … pursue God!"

Allow Room for Mistakes

If we don't allow room for the mistakes of others, we definitely won't allow room for our own mistakes, and we will be extremely hard on ourselves.

Beverly Flaxington, with *Psychology Today*, asks some hard but important questions that we must take time to think about:

Do you enjoy it when other people judge and critique you? Does it encourage you to thrive or boost your self-confidence? Would you tolerate it if someone bullied your child or harassed your friend? Without a doubt, these are painful experiences. So why let the voices in your own head do the same to you?

Why be your own bully? Because that is what you are if you incessantly self-criticize. No one knows you better than you do; no one knows what hurts you most, or how to attack your weaknesses in the meanest way possible.[32]

Why are we so hard on ourselves? What are we trying to accomplish?

Self-compassion is one of the most overlooked disciplines of humankind.

And the truth is, we have all done it; we have all had expectations of others and of ourselves that weren't kind, and honestly, weren't helpful. But in order to discover our resilience, we must learn how to cut our losses and move forward because failure can teach us so much for the future. I can say without a second thought that I learned so much more from my failures than I ever learned from my successes.

I remember being in a sparring match in Colorado Springs at The Taekwondo Nationals. The fighter was dirty, but she beat me fair and square. She beat the first girl in ten seconds flat (who also happened to be carried out on a stretcher). For me, it was a victory because I walked away, and although it was a slow walk, I walked. I always said she may have beat me in numbers, but she didn't beat me in spirit.

> **I can say without a second thought that I learned so much more from my failures than I ever learned from my successes.**

Overcoming Mistakes

We have all made mistakes, millions of them probably, and we have all been the victim of someone else's mistakes. There are often messes to clean up, forgiveness to both give and also receive, and humble conversations to be had. But in the end, moving forward is the goal.

It is actually the only way.

We may or may not get an apology from someone, but we must purpose and choose to forgive those who have hurt us, which can include ourselves.

Mistakes are going to happen in life, and we have to be able to release what has happened in order to move forward. Moving forward with a healthy mindset is how we allow our resilience to gain its strength in our lives.

The inability to accept something that isn't absolutely flawless is killing our society.

It keeps people from doing anything. It is paralyzing.

Overcoming Mindsets

Let's first look at a definition of the word mindset from *Psychology Today*: "A mindset is a belief that orients the way we handle situations — the way we sort out what is going on and what we should do. Our mindsets help us spot opportunities but they can [also] trap us in self-defeating cycles."[33]

Overcoming Criticism

This one can be hard. Words have extreme power in our lives. But we must be ok with hearing what someone has to say, knowing we have the power to agree with it or not.

Being heavily bothered by criticism is often a sign of perfectionism.

But criticism of others can't be avoided especially if you are stepping into new things that are different from those around you. It is healthy to not think of criticism as something to avoid rather, to realize it is a part of life's learning process.[34]

Sometimes we get discouraged because all we think about is what we have done wrong, but there are also emotional baggage, mindsets, mentalities, and things we are thinking about that get in the way.

And we must let those go.

What we don't want is to be discouraged by all that is inside our beautiful and somewhat complicated soul. God is so creative, detailed, and kind. He didn't make us complicated. He deliberately made us to have capacity beyond our human mind, so we don't want to get caught up with navel-gazing, which is looking inside yourself for all that is potentially wrong with you. It's not our job to "fix ourselves," but as the Apostle Paul said, *"we can forget what lies behind us and move forward toward what is ahead."* This letting go part is not always easy, but it is exactly what needs to happen in order to move forward with the ease and rest of God.

In becoming who you already are, which is excellent in every way, you are resilient, and through the eyes of Jesus Christ, you are perfect. As crazy as this may sound, when God looks at you, He already sees perfection because He sees a perfect Jesus that now lives inside you. So, if you have received Christ as your Savior, you have actually received His perfection. Choose to receive and you will know that He is so proud of who you are and all you have overcome.

The game-changer is when we realize that God already sees this perfection in us. When that happens, it causes us to drop our perfection facade, accept our human limitations, and allow God to do amazing things through us!

A Resilient Person Lets Go

Susan Biali, M.D., wrote for *Psychology Today* about the book "Grace for the Good Girl: Letting Go of the Try Hard Life":

> I'm just starting to fully realize what an impact the pressure to perform, please and be perfect has had, and continues to have, on my life. I've been aware of it for a long time and have made such progress from the days when I had to excel at anything and everything. I became addicted to praise and approval as a young child, and for most of my life cared more about doing what would make others proud or happy than what would truly light me up and nourish me. I believe this was a significant root of the depression I used to suffer from. There is still this undercurrent of performance, of needing to keep everyone happy, of wanting to be universally liked and

approved of (even by people who I might not be that fond of), to not cause anyone stress, discomfort or unhappiness through my choices. To want to be perfect.

So many of us are trying to live up to expectations or reputations. A good reputation is a good thing, but it goes bad when you start to feel that you can't be human. What if you just let yourself be your messy human self and trusted that all would be okay anyway? That your real self, with its full range of emotion and performance (from great to profoundly imperfect) is just fine. More than enough, actually.[35]

Below are some tips to help you cope with perfectionism:

- **Become aware of your negative self-dialogue.** Harsh and critical self-assessments reinforce perfectionism and procrastination.
- **Practice self-compassion.** When we are compassionate with ourselves, our fear of failure is not exaggerated. Mistakes are understood as being a natural and normal part of learning and life.
- **Take the time to examine whether your goals and expectations are attainable.** If they are not, give yourself permission to change them.
- **Break goals down into smaller steps.**
- **Examine your irrational fears of failure with a professional.** A professional can help with putting your irrational fears into perspective and help you to reach your full potential.[36]

▶

1-2 it's up to you!

Resilient Thought:

The game-changer is when you realize that because of Jesus, God already sees perfection in you. When that happens, it causes you to drop your perfection facade, accept your human limitations, and allow God to do amazing things through you!

1) What frustrations and disappointments do you need to let go of in order to move towards a better life?

2) What "impossible" standards have you set for your life, that you realize aren't from God, and are never going to benefit you?

A Resilient Person Loves to Share the Wealth

How to Be Generous in Every Way ▶

Shawn and Samantha walked away from the crowd of people with a flurry of emotions pulsating through their being. As a brother and sister who were now both in their late-40's, they hadn't even really had time to stop and process the events of the past few days. Samantha started the conversation with her older brother, "I'm not sure I ever knew someone who affected people the way that dad did. I mean, like so many people in so many different ways." Shawn responded with full-agreement, "I was thinking just now as the minister was praying to end the graveside service, I so badly want to reflect the same level of generosity in my life that dad did: with my money, in my relationships, with compassion and perspective in the way I encourage others—just all of it." The two siblings continued their tender exchange of praise for their father for the next few minutes, knowing that they had experienced and been given a front-row seat to greatness.

Chapter 12

▼

What you hold is unique. Not because your
circumstances are unique, rather because your perspective,
your upbringing, your values, your stage of life and your
personality all differ and have a unique story to tell.

Everything in your life plays into the way you handled
certain situations in life, and that combination for each person
is powerful.

You hold the power to help someone else by just being you
and by not being intimidated to bring value to others through
your life.

I love that.

What you've learned in life is priceless. Literally, you can't
put a price tag on the knowledge, insight, and wisdom you have
gained through all in which you have been through.

I applaud you. This journey is not always easy.

I believe one of the biggest lies that we are told in life is that
everyone knows what we know.

And that's simply not true.

It often feels like "what we know no one else would need."

We believe this lie because what we know seems like second
nature to us. It has become part of our value system and the
way in which we now see the world around us.

Best-selling books were born out of things that seemed kind of obvious to some.

Think for a minute about the legendary book *How to Win Friends and Influence People.*

For some, this book was life-changing. I remember large organizations buying it up for all their employees. I also remember some employees thinking that this content was kind of obvious and weren't sure why the company they worked for thought it was so revolutionary.

Why? Because for some, it was obvious, and for others, it was revolutionary.

We all wear different lenses. We all have different perspectives, different innate talents, different skill sets, and therefore, very different ways in which we understand the world around us.

We must find rest in the journey we have been on and know it is not the same as those around us.

The human condition is one that relates in many ways even if different paths are taken by each.

The paths seem similar with points of connection, somewhat like that of a spider web. Our understanding of life is like "the strand of spider silk"—lines or threads that cross each other at different points but no two being exactly the same.

> **We must find rest in the journey we have been on and know it is not the same as those around us.**

For this reason, we can all tell our stories of resilience and help different people, at different stages of life for different reasons. The point is that once the strands mesh together, they provide incredible strength.

Stories are important, that is how Hollywood became Hollywood. It's the story capital of the world. They have made gazillions of dollars writing stories not only to entertain people but also to inspire them.

We all hold a story in each us that will encourage, bring hope, and empower many others around us; we often just don't realize it.

You may think that your story is too similar to those around you, so why tell yours? But that is where the power lies. That is where the dynamite forms. The more real-life stories of conquerors like yourself, the better. The more faith is built in those who hear the stories that they can overcome if you did.

You are literally filling people with hope, just by being you.

And since there is nothing new under the sun, your problems won't be unique, but the journey you took to overcome them will be, and therein lies the power.

You are powerful and so is your story.

Look Differently

You may not feel like you've done that much to overcome in life, but I bet if you look back and process how things happened, you will see the turns you took, decisions you made, divine help you received, and you will start to see your story for what it is— compelling.

I didn't think my story had any power either, that was until I started telling it and people would say to me, "Andrea, you have a lot of knowledge that could help others." I didn't even realize people needed what I knew.

I bet the same is true for you.

You have a story that will inspire people, and I invite you to use it. I encourage you to realize the strength of your life and that which you have overcome.

And if writing a book sounds painful to you, don't worry, there is another way; there are several other ways.

For me, it was about being in touch with God to discover what He was asking me to do. God is not a cookie-cutter God. He is much the opposite. He is a very personal God and will walk you through anything, step by step, if you allow Him.

He will show you where and with who your story needs to be shared. And I believe that when we get to heaven we will more than likely meet people that shared their story with just a few that ended up having such a ripple effect that generations were changed.

It may be as simple as sharing your story of motherhood on the airplane with a young mother needing to know she is doing the right thing even though it feels like the hardest thing she has ever had to do.

It's doesn't need to be a big production. Your verbal story-telling is powerful.

Sherry Hamby, Ph.D., said in an article she wrote in *Psychology Today*:

I have been surprised at the power of emotional, autobiographical storytelling. Emotional, autobiographical storytelling means writing about events and people that have mattered to you in your own life--not just describing the facts of your lives. Research shows that even brief autobiographical storytelling exercises can have substantial impacts on psychological and physical health even months after the storytelling. Although in the dominant Western culture we often use writing to tell stories, I have also seen the power of oral storytelling. For example, oral storytelling is a major tool in many interventions developed by American Indian healers.[37]

Sharing the stories of your life can be one of the most rewarding things you do. In the Bible it says that we overcome the enemy (the Father of lies and all evil in the world) by the blood of the lamb (which is Jesus dying on the cross for all mankind) and the word of our testimony.

**It's doesn't need to be a big production.
Your verbal storytelling is powerful.**

A testimony is a story. And our stories are meant to be told.
It's interesting how the most powerful being in the world said that it would be our stories that would help overcome evil. Wow!
And it isn't only said by the Bible, but Psychology Today affirms this same notion that storytelling is a lot more powerful than many realize.

A Way of Healing

Storytelling of any kind can be healing not only for those who read it but also for those who write it. Whether your story is recorded in a book, a newspaper, on a public blog, or in your private journal, writing has the power to transform your own life. Gloria Kempton writes:

> *The Hero's Journey Prison Writing Project* program aims to assist inmates in challenging the perceptions they have of themselves as victims/perpetrators and encourages and supports a paradigm shift in their thinking to that of the hero archetype—one of taking responsibility for the journey they find themselves on and how to make the most of it in terms of self-development and internal discovery. At its core, this program is about each person learning to transform negative beliefs about himself into a more positive self-image, therefore taking responsibility for his own life and actions. The Hero's Journey is a powerful metaphorical storytelling tool we use to facilitate this process. With an emphasis on the exploration of Joseph Campbell's work addressing the structure of the hero's journey and Chris Vogler's adaptation of that structure in *The Writer's Journey*, the Hero's Journey Prison Writing Project introduces prisoners to an alternative structure for analyzing their personal story, prior to prison, while in prison and in thinking about their release. ...

- The mythologist, Joseph Campbell, first wrote about

The Hero's Journey as a design for storytelling in 1949.
It's an age-old storycrafting tool still effectively used
by modern writers, like George Lucas with Star Wars.

- Christopher Vogler, a former Hollywood story consultant,
adapted these ideas in his bestseller, The Writer's
Journey, published in 1992. Vogler came to realize
that The Hero's Journey was not only a solid blueprint
for telling stories, it was a useful set of guidelines for
navigating almost any challenging experience.

- Now Gloria Kempton, Director of The Hero's
Journey Prison Writing Project, in The Outlaw's Journey
Correspondence Course, introduces this concept to
writers behind bars. While helping them strengthen
their writing skills, she compassionately guides them
through a transformative process, giving them the
opportunity to honestly look at their own life's
journey with its internal and external struggles,
and become the Hero they were always meant to be.[38]

I also remember the movie *Freedom Writers* where the teacher
(Hilary Swank) finds herself in a class of at-risk teenagers deemed
incapable of learning. Instead of giving up, she inspired her students
to take an interest in their education and planning their
future. She assigned reading material that related to their lives
and encouraged them all to keep journals.

She used stories of others like Anne Frank who suffered
like they had in their young lives to earn their trust, and then
she bought them composition books to record their own stories

of abuse, like seeing their friends die and being evicted. She compiled their journals into book form and titled it *The Freedom Writers Diary*.

This teacher successfully prepared numerous high school students to graduate high school and attend college; for many, they were first in their families to do so.

There is something powerful on both sides of any story: your healing and the healing of others.

When you invest in the life and future of others, the payout is multifold:

1. Brings deep meaning and satisfaction.
2. It takes your eyes off your own issues—things that seem like mountains are often reduced to mole holes.
3. It builds empathy and understanding for people that are different than you.

A friend of mine who has worked with some of the most influential personalities in the world said that people who stay connected to others while they are doing their life work become more forgiving and less idealistic. For example, those personalities that speak more from a platform but are not connected to people during the day to day responsibilities seem to be more idealistic, which often isn't helpful.

There is something powerful on both sides of any story: your healing and the healing of others

He says personally investing while teaching from a platform will keep you more in touch and more forgiving of others. I couldn't agree more.

The more we can see the real story the better; that is why the show *Undercover Boss* is so interesting. Once the leader sees what his people are dealing with, he can have more empathy for their process, and not only that, but he also has the power to improve parts of their process.

Empathy to Heal and Help Others

What we go through we have the power to speak into. Why? Because people will listen to us if they know they can trust us because we have a better understanding of how they feel more than anyone else around them.

Forbes Magazine says that a major skill set they are looking for in leaders today is empathy.

The writer goes on to say that "…empathy is a learned ability, not a personality trait. Empathy builds trust. Trust and respect are the foundation for every healthy relationship…"[39]

We haven't all been through the same things in life; therefore, we often can't understand what others are going through unless we can put ourselves in their situations, which is the basis of empathy.

But when you have personally experienced a challenging situation, you are able to have an intense understanding of what the person in front of you is dealing with, and that makes you powerful in the situation, maybe more than anyone else in their life.

Anything you go through changes your perspective and ability to help others in that same situation.

You have been through the fire, and the world needs your empathy.

Jesus came to see what it was like on earth, He wanted to go through what we have to go through, so we would know that there was One who truly understood all the pain we have suffered. He then endured the worst pain that anyone could on the cross for us to receive reconciliation to the God of the universe who could redeem and restore all that had been stolen.

We often don't recognize the significant value of our experiences to help another. I must implore you to realize that what you hold in your hand—the pain, the victories, the hope and the process—will ignite and unleash those around you.

Your story is significant and somebody else needs to hear it.

When you share the wealth of what you have learned in life, it will cause the cycle of defeat to be broken in you and others.

There are multiple ways to share your story; you can be as creative as you wish. I would propose anything from writing poetry, song lyrics, or inspirational quotes, to drawing, painting, taking photos or filming videos. Whatever the creative outlet, let it be authentically you:

You have an authentic voice. You can make a difference for yourself and others by sharing your experiences and perspective. What has helped? What hasn't? What has been most discouraging? What has given you hope? There are all sorts of things you know that other people want to know—but the one thing they want more than anything is to know they are not alone.[40]

I have talked a lot about the Bible, but I want to leave you with what the science of psychology has to say about sharing your story. I love how they talk about peace and hope because those are values of the Kingdom of God and when the Bible and psychology come together, well, I get excited. I don't believe it was ever supposed to be separate. God created humans and psychology, which is simply the study of humans. Why wouldn't they agree? Especially in this area of peace and hope.

> **When you share the wealth of what you have learned in life, it will cause the cycle of defeat to be broken in you and others.**

In the article *Resilience and…4 Benefits to Sharing Your Story*, new insights into resilience can help everyone get better at bouncing back.

The author tells us that the last of the four benefits of sharing our story as tied to being resilient is:

Finding peace, finding hope

What's the difference between someone who has achieved resilience and someone who has not? One important difference is a sense of well-being. People who have found their voice, shared their story, and reaffirmed their values often find a sense of peace and a hopefulness that they did not have before.

"Just actually sitting down and writing probably helped me find that, that peace...."

"I got closure and I let go of the <u>anger</u>. And I think when you let go of the anger you are freer.... Anger holds you back and I think once I read it and turned it in, I was like, 'It is what it is.' (<u>laughter</u>) It was like a chapter that was being closed and I started planning for my future."

For those of you who may still be struggling to overcome challenges or difficult times, one of our participants said if she could pass something on now, she'd say be hopeful. In her words:

"Your story hasn't been written yet. The final chapter hasn't been written yet." [41]

I couldn't agree more.

The final chapter of your life has not been written, and you hold an author's pencil to help you write that ending. You may base your future on your past, but that is not the best plan. The best plan is to have hope for a future that is is still being written.

So, let's move forward and be our true selves to all those around us because they are not waiting for another me, they are waiting for an incredible, vulnerable and empowered you!

▶

1-2 it's up to you!

Resilient Thought:

You hold a story and value in you that will encourage, bring hope, and empower many others around you; it's now time to realize it and do something with it.

1) What are at least 3-4 areas that you are willing to share with others in order to add value to their lives?

2) What can you do right now to begin to live generously with your time, energy and money?

What Now

I've given you the tools that can make a difference in your life.

My challenge to you is simply this, "What are you going to do with them?"

You can keep staying in cycles of discouragement and defeat.

Or...

You can rebuild your thinking and ultimately your life, by making the choice to declare daily, "I Am Resilent."

I believe you'll choose the latter, and your life will never be the same because of it.

Keep me posted on your journey...

andrea@iamresilient.net

Your Decision

I have had the privilege of traveling to some amazing places, and have spoken to thousands of people, from all walks of life. Although we all seem so different, one from the other – almost everyone strives for the same basic necessities, the same basic human dignity and the same sense of purpose in our lives.

For me, I found my purpose by having a living relationship with Jesus Christ. That relationship is the bedrock foundation of everything that is good, and has allowed me to see God's Promise and God's Purpose for my life. Would you like to give your life to Jesus? Would you like to completely and absolutely invite the living Christ into your heart? If you have never asked Jesus into your heart before, then there is no better day than today. And there is no better time than now. All you have to do is believe and read this very simple prayer out loud:

"Lord Jesus, I confess with my mouth and believe in my heart, that you died on a cross and that you rose again.
I receive your forgiveness for of all my sins
Thank you that you love me.
In Jesus Name ... Amen!"

And with that simple prayer my dear sister or brother in Christ... you are now part of the family of God!

EndNotes

1 Diane Coutu, "How Resilience Works," *HBR.org*, May 2002

2 Diane Coutu, "How Resilience Works," *HBR.org*, May 2002

3 Hara Estroff Marano, "The Art of Resilience," *Psychologytoday.com*, May 1, 2003

4 Diane Coutu, "How Resilience Works," *HBR.org*, May 2002

5 Valorie Burton, "4 Things Resilient People Do!", *Valorieburton,com*

6 C. Kavin Rowe, "Cultivating resilience in Christ-shaped leaders," *Faithandleadership.com*, April 23, 2012

7 Martin Zwilling, "How To Build Your Resilience To Be An Entrepreneur," *Forbes.com*, July 28, 2015

8 Denise Foley, "Resilience can get you through life's trials," *Nbcnews.com*, December 24, 2007

9 Alex Lickerman, M.D., "Why We Laugh," *Psychologytoday.com*, January 23, 2011

10 David DiSalvo, "Six Science-Based Reasons Why Laughter Is The Best Medicine," *Forbes,com*, June 5, 2017

11 Steve Shirley, "What does it mean to have revival?," *Jesusalive.cc*

12 Steve Backlund. *Let's Just Laugh at That*. Kindle Edition. PG. 11

13 Matthew Toren, "6 Thoughts on Why Facing Your Fears Could Help You Achieve Massive Success," *Entrepreneur.com*, November 13, 2015

14 Noam Shpancer, Ph.D., "Overcoming Fear: The Only Way Out is Through," *Psychologytoday.com*, September 20, 2010

15 Eric Barker, "10 Ways to Boost Emotional Intelligence,

Backed By Research," *Time.com*, April 26, 2016

16 Jill Suttie, "Four Ways Social Support Makes You More Resilient," *Greatergood.berkeley.edu*, November 13, 2017

17 Robert D. Putnam, "Bowling Alone: The Collapse and Revival of American Community," *Bowlingalone.com*

18 Hari, Johann. (2015, June). Everything you think you know about addiction is wrong. Retrieved from https://www.ted.com/talks/johann_hari_everything_you_think_you_know_about_addiction_is_wrong

19 Johann Hari, "The Likely Cause of Addiction Has Been Discovered, and It Is Not What You Think", *Huffingtonpost.com*, January 20, 2015

20 Johann Hari, "The Likely Cause of Addiction Has Been Discovered, and It Is Not What You Think", *Huffingtonpost.com*, January 20, 2015

21 Johann Hari, "The Likely Cause of Addiction Has Been Discovered, and It Is Not What You Think", *Huffingtonpost.com*, January 20, 2015

22 Jill Suttie, "Four Ways Social Support Makes You More Resilient," *Greatergood.berkeley.edu*, November 13, 2017

23 Henry Cloud, Ph.D., "The Simple Scoop on Boundaries," *Cloudtownsend.com*, July 30, 2000

24 Rich Fernandez, "5 Ways to Boost Your Resilience at Work," *HBR.org*, June 27, 2016

25 Eric Barker, "10 Ways to Boost Emotional Intelligence, Backed By Research," *Time.com*, April 26, 2016

26 Preston Ni, MSBA, "How To Spot and Stop Narcissists," *Psychologytoday.com*, January 4, 2015

27 Kimberly Yam, "10 Facts That Prove Helping Others Is A Key To Achieving Happiness," *Huffingtonpost.com*, March 20, 2015

28 Preston Ni, MSBA, "10 Signs That You're in a Relationship with A Narcissist," *Psychologytoday.com*, September 14, 2014

29 Thomas G. Plante, Ph.D., "Helping Others Offers Surprising Benefits," *Psychologytoday.com*, July 2, 2012

30 Tara Parker-Pope, "How to Build Resilience in Mid-Life," *NYTimes.com*, July 25, 2017

31 Charles F. Stanley, "Life Principle 6: The Principle of Sowing and Reaping," *Intouch.org*, July 6, 2014

32 Beverly D. Flaxington, "5 Ways to Stop Beating Yourself Up," *Psychologytoday.com*, May 8, 2015

33 Gary Klein, Ph.D., "Seeing What Others Don't," *Psychologytoday.com*

34 Adam Sicinski, "How To Handle Criticism And Bounce Back Feeling More Empowered," *blog.iqmatrix.com*

35 Susan Biali, M.D., "Let Go of Perfectionism, Pleasing and Performing," *Psychologytoday.com*, October 29, 2013

36 Paula Durlofsky, Ph.D., "How to Let Go of Perfectionism," *Psychcentral.com*

37 Sherry Hamby, Ph.D., "Resilience and … 4 Benefits to Sharing Your Story," *Psychologytoday.com*, September 3, 2013

38 Gloria Kempton, "Hero's Journey Prison Writing Project," *Glokemp2.wordpress.com*

39 Melinda Fouts, Ph.D., "Empathy: A Major Skillset in Demand for Leaders," *Forbes.com*, February 13, 2018

40 "Share Your Story," www.nami.org

41 Sherry Hamby, Ph.D., "Resilience and … 4 Benefits to Sharing Your Story," *Psychologytoday.com*, September 3, 2013

andreathompson.org

Andrea Thompson

BLOG   ABOUT   PODCAST   STORE   **GET STARTED TODAY!**

YOU CAN OVERCOME!

In health. In life.

GET STARTED TODAY!

Get my eBook with the behind-the-scenes strategies I used to overcome cancer!

YES, ANDREA, I WANT TO DISCOVER HOW YOU OVERCAME THE DEADLY DISEASE IN 90 DAYS:

Email Address

DOWNLOAD NOW

Find more great tools and resources to encourage you in YOUR journey, including:

- fully downloadable digital resources
- content-rich blog
- weekly podcast
  ...and more